TEEN RIGHTS AND FREEDOMS

| The Internet

Teen Rights and Freedoms

I The Internet

Cynthia A. Bily
Book Editor

GREENHAVEN PRESS
A part of Gale, Cengage Learning

GALE
CENGAGE Learning·

Detroit • New York • San Francisco • New Haven, Conn • Waterville, Maine • London

Elizabeth Des Chenes, *Managing Editor*

© 2012 Greenhaven Press, a part of Gale, Cengage Learning

Gale and Greenhaven Press are registered trademarks used herein under license.

For more information, contact:
Greenhaven Press
27500 Drake Rd.
Farmington Hills, MI 48331-3535
Or you can visit our Internet site at gale.cengage.com.

For product information and technology assistance, contact us at:

Gale Customer Support, 1-800-877-4253.
For permission to use material from this text or product, submit all requests online at www.cengage.com/permissions.

Further permissions questions can be emailed to permissionrequest@cengage.com.

Articles in Greenhaven Press anthologies are often edited for length to meet page requirements. In addition, original titles of these works are changed to clearly present the main thesis and to explicitly indicate the author's opinion. Every effort is made to ensure the Greenhaven Press accurately reflects the original intent of the authors. Every effort has been made to trace the owners of copyrighted material.

Cover Image © EDHAR/ShutterStock.com

LIBRARY OF CONGRESS CATALOGING-IN-PUBLICATION DATA

The Internet / Cynthia A. Bily, book editor.
   p. cm. -- (Teen rights and freedoms)
   Includes bibliographical references and index.
   ISBN 978-0-7377-5829-0 (hardcover)
1. Internet and teenagers--United States. 2. Internet--Law and legislation--United States. 3. Teenagers--Legal status, laws, etc.--United States. 4. Libraries and teenagers--United States. 5. Internet--Access control--United States. 6. Internet--Safety measures. 7. United States. Telecommunications Act of 1996. 8. Cyberbullying--United States. 9. Computer crimes--Prevention. I. Bily, Cynthia A.
   KF390.5.C6I55 2012
   343.7309'944--dc23
                    2011043215

Contents

The American Library Association, interpreting its own Library Bill of Rights, states that minors must be allowed the same access to the Internet as adults have and must be taught to use the Internet wisely and safely.

An attorney for the Pennsylvania School Boards Association argues that websites created away from school can be disruptive within school boundaries and should be punishable just like on-campus speech.

Foreword

"In the truest sense freedom cannot be bestowed, it must be achieved."

Franklin D. Roosevelt,
September 16, 1936

The notion of children and teens having rights is a relatively recent development. Early in American history, the head of the household—nearly always the father—exercised complete control over the children in the family. Children were legally considered to be the property of their parents. Over time, this view changed, as society began to acknowledge that children have rights independent of their parents, and that the law should protect young people from exploitation. By the early twentieth century, more and more social reformers focused on the welfare of children, and over the ensuing decades advocates worked to protect them from harm in the workplace, to secure public education for all, and to guarantee fair treatment for youths in the criminal justice system. Throughout the twentieth century, rights for children and teens—and restrictions on those rights—were established by Congress and reinforced by the courts. Today's courts are still defining and clarifying the rights and freedoms of young people, sometimes expanding those rights and sometimes limiting them. Some teen rights are outside the scope of public law and remain in the realm of the family, while still others are determined by school policies.

Each volume in the Teen Rights and Freedoms series focuses on a different right or freedom and offers an anthology of key essays and articles on that right or freedom and the responsibilities that come with it. Material within each volume is drawn from a diverse selection of primary and secondary sources—journals, magazines, newspapers, nonfiction books, organization newsletters, position papers, speeches, and government documents, with a particular emphasis on Supreme Court and lower court decisions. Volumes also include first-person narratives from young people and others involved in teen rights issues, such as parents and educators. The material is selected and arranged to highlight all the major social and legal controversies relating to the right or freedom under discussion. Each selection is preceded by an introduction that provides context and background. In many cases, the essays point to the difference between adult and teen rights, and why this difference exists.

Many of the volumes cover rights guaranteed under the Bill of Rights and how these rights are interpreted and protected in regard to children and teens, including freedom of speech, freedom of the press, due process, and religious rights. The scope of the series also encompasses rights or freedoms, whether real or perceived, relating to the school environment, such as electronic devices, dress, Internet policies, and privacy. Some volumes focus on the home environment, including topics such as parental control and sexuality.

Numerous features are included in each volume of Teen Rights and Freedoms:

- An annotated **table of contents** provides a brief summary of each essay in the volume and highlights court decisions and personal narratives.

- An **introduction** specific to the volume topic gives context for the right or freedom and its impact on daily life.

- A brief **chronology** offers important dates associated with the right or freedom, including landmark court cases.

- **Primary sources**—including personal narratives and court decisions—are among the varied selections in the anthology.

- **Illustrations**—including photographs, charts, graphs, tables, statistics, and maps—are closely tied to the text and chosen to help readers understand key points or concepts.

- An annotated list of **organizations to contact** presents sources of additional information on the topic.
- A **for further reading** section offers a bibliography of books, periodical articles, and Internet sources for further research.
- A comprehensive subject **index** provides access to key people, places, events, and subjects cited in the text.

Each volume of Teen Rights and Freedoms delves deeply into the issues most relevant to the lives of teens: their own rights, freedoms, and responsibilities. With the help of this series, students and other readers can explore from many angles the evolution and current expression of rights both historic and contemporary.

Introduction

> *"For many parents and educators, the Internet is a lot like an unpredictable and street-smart friend. Adults want to trust it, but they are uncertain how to protect their children from the new and foreign ideas it can provide access to."*
>
> Todd Savage, *"Beware the Cyber Censors,"* The Advocate

Since the Internet became widely available in the 1990s, parents, educators and lawmakers have struggled to balance the right of teenagers to use the Internet with the desire to protect them from harm. On one hand, teens have derived benefits from the Internet that even the most grudging adult must admire. Teens have found that going online can help them do research and other educational tasks more easily and in greater depth than earlier generations could imagine. They have also used social networking to make friends with other young people around the world, to rally support for interesting and important causes, to work collaboratively on creative projects, and even to stay in touch with their grandparents. But with this easy access comes threats that worry adults: widely distributed texts and images can include pornographic and extremely violent material; new friends found on social networking sites sometimes turn out to be dangerous predators; and the anonymity of the Internet can encourage young people (and, often, older people) to make unkind or threatening comments they would never make in person. Some adults are concerned that the Internet exposes young people to ideas and opinions about religion, sexuality, politics and other issues that go against parents' teachings. To respond to these perceived dangers, in the mid-1990s adults began to make laws and policies restricting teens' Internet access.

Thus far, attempts to regulate what teens may do on the Internet have been largely unsuccessful. The First Amendment to the United States Constitution prohibits making laws "abridging the freedom of speech," and this has generally been thought to include what people create on the Internet. Congress has tried several times to write laws that keep people from publishing controversial materials where children might see them, or that allow schools to punish students for creating insulting websites, but these laws have been struck down by the courts because they were found to violate the rights and freedoms guaranteed by the First Amendment. School administrators and parents have tried from the beginning to establish their own policies to keep teens away from trouble on the Internet, but more often than not these policies have been ineffective.

In the early days many adults were simply unaware of the possibilities of the Internet. As often happens, young people found ways to use and abuse the new technology, and it took adults months or years to discover what teens were doing and regulate their activities. In 1998, a Chicago school district technology director, Kenneth A. Wiseman, told a writer for *Education Week*, "Our principals have been very hands-offish about the Internet. Many principals don't understand what the Internet is." Today, principals and other adults know what the Internet is, but they often do not know what teens are doing online until they discover too late that teens have been illegally downloading music and movies, using social media to mock or bully others, posting sexually revealing pictures of themselves, plagiarizing school work, or leaving themselves vulnerable to adults who might wish them harm.

The fact that young people often know more about technology than their parents and teachers makes it difficult for adults to make laws and policies to protect them from making mistakes with technology. For example, in the year 2000, Congress passed the Children's Online Privacy Protection Act (COPPA), intending to prevent website operators from gathering personal information about children under the age of thirteen. This is why the privacy policy for the social media website Facebook states, "If you are under age 13, please do not attempt to register for Facebook or provide any personal information about yourself to us. If we learn that we have collected personal information from a child under age 13, we will delete that information as quickly as possible." However, a survey conducted by *Consumer Reports* magazine and published in June 2011 found that 7.5 million children younger than thirteen lied about their age and used Facebook in the previous year anyway, including 5 million aged ten or younger—and their parents were mostly unaware of or unconcerned about what these young people were doing. Other websites offer instructions for Internet users who want to get around the filtering software used by schools and libraries. It is natural for adults to want to protect young people, just as it is natural for teens to resist even well-meaning restrictions.

The issues will only become more complex as technology becomes more integrated, more portable, and more available. With even inexpensive cell phones able to connect to the Internet, with most homes, schools, libraries and coffee shops equipped with personal computers, and with many video games incorporating online activities, adults will find it harder to restrict what teens are doing online. Many librarians and teachers have urged parents and lawmakers to focus on educating teens to be smart Internet users, rather than to continue crafting new rules. In 2011 Kim Patton, president of the Young Adult Library Services Association, stressed this approach in *YALS*, the organization's journal: "We need to talk to [teens] about their rights and responsibilities. . . . We need to impart the knowledge that along with these great gadgets and wonderful tools comes the responsibility to use them wisely and to become good citizens and stewards of a digital environment." Key court decisions and commentary on teens and the Internet are further explored in *Teen Rights and Freedoms: The Internet*.

Chronology

1791

The Bill of Rights is adopted by the United States. The first of the ten Amendments reads: "Congress shall make no law respecting an establishment of religion, or prohibiting the free exercise thereof; or abridging the freedom of speech, or of the press; or the right of the people peaceably to assemble, and to petition the Government for a redress of grievances."

1969

In *Tinker v. Des Moines Independent Community School District* the US Supreme Court establishes the First Amendment rights of students enrolled in public school, commenting, "It can hardly be argued that either students or teachers shed their constitutional rights to freedom of speech or expression at the schoolhouse gate."

1986

In *Bethel v. Fraser* the US Supreme Court holds that school officials may regulate lewd and offensive speech occurring at school.

1996

Congress passes the Communications Decency Act (CDA), its first attempt to regulate Internet pornography. Part of a broader Telecom Reform Bill, the Act makes it illegal to knowingly transmit "obscene or indecent" material to anyone under eighteen years of age.

1997 The US Supreme Court rules in *Reno v. American Civil Liberties Union* and in *American Library Association v. US Department of Justice* that the Communications Decency Act is unconstitutional, finding that the provisions regulating "indecent transmission" and "patently offensive display" violate the First Amendment's guarantee of freedom of speech.

1998 Congress passes the Child Online Protection Act (COPA), another attempt to regulate Internet pornography. Under COPA, commercial pornography sites must require a credit card for access or use other means to keep minors from gaining access to explicit content.

1999 The Third Circuit Court of Appeals rules that the US Department of Justice may not enforce COPA, largely because it finds that filtering software can achieve the goal of preventing minors from gaining access to pornography without burdensome laws. COPA is debated in the courts for another decade, and is struck down again by the Appeals Court in 2003, 2006 and 2008. In 2009, the US Supreme Court effectively ends the debate by refusing to hear the case.

2000
The Children's Online Privacy Protection Act (COPPA), passed by Congress in 1998, goes into effect. It regulates the personal information that website operators may collect from children under the age of thirteen.

2001
In *A&M Records v. Napster* the Ninth Circuit Court of Appeals holds that the peer-to-peer file sharing Internet service Napster "knowingly encourages and assists the infringement of plaintiffs' copyrights."

2002
In *J.S. v. Bethlehem Area School District* the Supreme Court of Pennsylvania holds that school officials may punish a student for offensive and derogatory comments on a website created away from school.

2003
In *United States et al. v. American Library Association, Inc. et al.,* the US Supreme Court upholds the Children's Internet Protection Act (CIPA) of 2001. It requires public schools and libraries with Internet access funded by the federal government to use filtering software to restrict minors' access to pornography.

2007
In *Layshock v. Hermitage School District* a US District Court judge rules that school officials do not have the right to punish a student for a website he

created off-campus to make fun of his school principal. The judge writes, "Public schools are vital institutions, but their reach is not unlimited."

2009
Twenty states have laws intended to combat cyberbullying. At the federal level Representative Linda Sánchez of California introduces the Megan Meier Cyberbullying Prevention Act, but Congress does not act on it.

2009
On behalf of a school librarian and several students, the American Civil Liberties Union sues two Tennessee school districts in federal court, charging that the districts' filtering software unfairly restricts access to information about lesbian, gay, bisexual and transgendered (LGBT) people. As a result, all school districts in Tennessee agree to stop the practice.

2011
The US Third Circuit Court of Appeals rehears *J.S. v. Bethlehem Area School District* and *Layshock v. Hermitage School District,* finding in both cases that schools may not discipline students for online speech that "originated outside of the schoolhouse, did not disturb the school environment and was not related to any school sponsored event."

> *"From suspension, lawsuit, and criminal charges to being a victim of a sexual predator, kids are encountering serious problems."*

Understanding the Legal Issues of Teen Internet Use

Patrick E. Corbett

In the following viewpoint, law professor Patrick Corbett outlines how some of the common ways that teens use the Internet can lead them to commit crimes—or to be victims of crimes. Often, he argues, teens do not realize that what they are doing might be dangerous or illegal, because young people are so comfortable with online interactions that they tend not to stop and question them. But according to Corbett, who uses examples from the laws of Michigan, seemingly innocent activities like sending e-mails, creating pages on social networks, or even accessing WiFi from the backyard could be criminal offenses. Corbett teaches criminal law, criminal procedure, and computer crimes at Thomas M. Cooley Law School in Lansing, Michigan. For more than two years, he investigated and prosecuted federal and state Internet and computer-related crimes for the Michigan Attorney General's Office.

Every day across the United States people take advantage of the vast resources of the Internet and high-technology devices. From software that simplifies electronic data storage and retrieval to devices that facilitate immediate and direct communication, our high-tech society has some fantastic tools to use. According to the Pew Internet and American Life Project, as of December 2007, 75 percent of US adults use the Internet and 92 percent report sending e-mail. These figures are even higher for the younger age groups. It might be simpler to list those *not* online: infants, some senior citizens, and a handful of others.

Without a doubt, the technology is amazing; it's not surprising there are so many active users. This usage, however, is not without risks. Many are so enamored with the technology that security concerns are often overlooked. In addition, legislatures across the country are passing laws criminalizing conduct involving usage of both the Internet and high-technology devices. Is the public keeping up with the laws? How about our middle schoolers, teens, and young adults? Do they have any idea that what they are doing could get them suspended, expelled, sued, or prosecuted? Do they know when they are victims of crime? Do they know when they have committed a crime?

Using various realistic hypotheticals and Michigan law as a guide, this article will explore how teens and young adults are getting into trouble, both as victims and as criminal perpetrators. This information is fundamentally important to making well-informed decisions about how to use the Internet and high-technology devices. Hopefully, greater awareness will lead to more responsible usage of the incredible technology available to all today.

Kids Are Getting into Trouble

What one does online is not anonymous. People are watching: friends, family, police, crooks, sexual predators, school officials, universities, employers, potential employers, and people contemplating a lawsuit. The combination of these "watchers" with a youth culture that encourages sharing of personal details on the Internet and through an assortment of high-tech devices has resulted in teens getting into trouble in a wide variety of ways:

- Twenty California middle school students were suspended for "viewing" graphic threats against a classmate on the MySpace.com Web site.

- Twenty Michigan high-schoolers received a two-week suspension from sports, a dance, and other activities after school officials saw images of the students drinking alcohol in their online journals.

- "Police in the central Connecticut city of Middletown suspect that as many as seven girls were recently assaulted by men they met on MySpace."[1]

- Authorities charged a 28-year-old man with luring a 13-year-old boy into an online child pornography business after the teen posted a "photo on a webcam exchange in the hope of making friends."[2]

- A *Washington Post* article highlighted how teens on social network sites are "easy targets" of thieves because they are "more trusting" and "less security-conscious."

- "Two [Novato, California] teenage boys were arrested on charges of possessing 'destructive devices' after a video allegedly showing the duo firebombing an empty airplane hangar was posted online at MySpace.com. . . . [P]olice officers stationed at each middle and high school in Novato regularly surf the MySpace site for signs that local teenagers may be involved in criminal activity such as drug or alcohol use, sexual assault or vandalism."[3]

- Authorities used a recently passed anti-terrorism law to charge a 12-year-old Michigan girl after she "sent out Internet messages threatening to bomb her Chippewa Valley school."[4]

- Harvard Business School indicated "it is rejecting applications from 119 would-be students it accused of hacking into a Web site to learn if they were accepted before the sending of official notifications."[5]

- The University of Dayton found that 42 percent of employers in their database that responded to a survey stated they "would consider factoring a Facebook profile into their hiring decision."[6]

- "A Pennsylvania school principal has filed a lawsuit against four former students, claiming they falsely portrayed him as a pot smoker, beer guzzler and pornography lover and sullied his reputation through mock MySpace profiles."[7]

- A court upheld a state "law that makes parents liable for the costs of crimes committed by their juvenile children."[8]

- A 15-year-old teen is charged in Canada with the criminal offense of "personation after allegedly posing as a school teacher on Facebook, a social networking site."[9]

From suspension, lawsuit, and criminal charges to being a victim of a sexual predator, kids are encountering serious problems. How do the criminal laws address what teens are doing online? The criminal laws both *protect* teens and could be used to *prosecute* teens. . . .

Unauthorized Access to a Computer System

George wants to know if a private college accepted him, so he uses his high school's computer system and figures out how to peek in the private college's computer system. He finds out that he is accepted! In the process, he causes no damage to the computer system of either school. A crime?

Michigan law criminalizes the intentional and "unauthorized" (or by "exceeding valid authorization") access to "a computer program, computer, computer system, or computer network" to acquire, alter, damage, delete, or destroy property or "otherwise use the service of a computer program, computer,

computer system, or computer network." This offense is punishable by up to five years imprisonment, regardless of any amount of loss. In other words, no damage to the computer or computer system is needed; one needs only to "otherwise use the service" to be facing a five-year felony. . . .

Unauthorized Access to Another's WiFi

After school, 17-year-old Harold brings his laptop with WiFi capacity to Jim's house. Jim's computer is not working, and they need to get some information from a Web site. Harold takes his computer into the backyard and turns on his computer to search for a wireless computer system that he can use to access the Internet. He finds that the neighbor two houses away has left his wireless system insecure and that he can access the Internet through the neighbor's system. Without asking the neighbor for consent, Harold uses the neighbor's Internet access, he gets the information he needs, and they continue with their homework. A crime? Is accessing someone else's wireless Internet connection to surf the Internet a problem under the law?

Once again, Michigan law addresses this situation. The same statute that jammed up George . . . could cause problems for Harold (and, using principles of accomplice liability, possibly Jim). Certainly, Harold "accessed" a "computer system." He did it "intentionally"; he did not access the Internet by mistake or accident. The only real legal issue is whether his access was "unauthorized" or whether he "exceeded valid authorization." Arguably, he was not authorized to use the neighbor's system. Just because, technologically, Harold can get into the neighbor's system does not mean that he is *authorized* to use the neighbor's system. . . .

Sexual Predators

Sally, 13, is updating her Xanga blog site and she gets an instant message from a male with the screen name "Heybaby." Over a series of communications, Heybaby and Sally become friends.

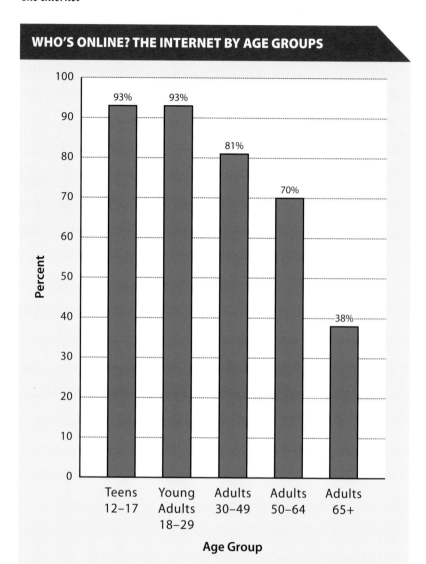

WHO'S ONLINE? THE INTERNET BY AGE GROUPS

Taken from: Amanda Lenhart, Kristen Purcell, Aaron Smith, and Kathryn Zickhur, "Social Media and Young Adults," Pew Internet and American Life Project, February 3, 2010.

Heybaby convinces Sally to meet at the local McDonald's, and after buying her a chocolate shake, he tries to force her into his car. Sally has taken karate lessons and is able to defend herself, and she breaks away. A subsequent search of Heybaby's car reveals the presence of a teddy bear, a rose, rope, condoms, and a digital camera. A crime?

Across the country, these types of incidents have been prosecuted as computer-related criminal sexual conduct offenses. . . .

Quite clearly, there is a downside to our teens' prolific and unguarded usage of the various high-tech ways of communicating. Awareness of the potential consequences of this conduct can help prevent some problems. To the extent that our kids are victimized, however, law enforcement can help. Internet crimes against children task forces exist in nearly every state. These task forces are comprised of local, state, and federal law enforcement officers who are actively pursuing these types of cases and are available to help our child victims. . . .

Stalking

Amanda sends five separate e-mails to Sydney telling Sydney that she is going to "mutilate her" if Sydney doesn't stay away from Amanda's boyfriend Jack. After the fifth e-mail, Sydney is so upset that she misses a week of school. A criminal violation?

Michigan law criminalizes a willful "course of conduct" involving "unconsented contact" with "another individual" that would make a reasonable person feel frightened or harassed and that actually causes the victim to feel frightened or harassed. Commonly referred to as "stalking," this offense is a misdemeanor punishable by up to one year in prison. How bad do the e-mails have to be to make someone feel harassed under the law? In general, due to the "reasonable person" language in the statute, the language needs to be bad enough that the average person would be upset. . . .

Amanda sent enough e-mails to satisfy the requirement for a "course of conduct"; the e-mails constituted "unconsented contact" in that Sydney did not ask to be sent these e-mails; the e-mails actually caused Sydney to feel frightened as exhibited by her missing a week of school; and a reasonable person would also be frightened by another's repeated assertion of a desire

The question of whether accessing a neighbor's unsecure WiFi is a crime has been addressed by some courts. © Christopher Robbins/Riser/Getty Images.

to "mutilate." Arguably, Amanda could be facing two separate criminal charges (one misdemeanor and one felony) due to her e-mail conduct.

Cyberbullying

Robert sends several instant messages to those on his e-mail "buddy" list that state classmate Eric cheated on an exam (when Eric did not and Robert knew that he did not). He encourages them to hassle Eric for cheating. A few send nasty e-mails to Eric. Eric is so upset that he misses three days of school. A crime? What if this is posted to Robert's Facebook site? . . .

Assuming that the prosecutor chose to take the case, it appears that Robert could be facing a felony charge whether he sent instant messages or posted the information on his Facebook site. He posted the messages through a medium of communication; it appears that he intended that the posting would result in harassment to Eric in that he knew Eric did not cheat but he encouraged others to hassle him as if he had; the posting of the message would cause a reasonable person to feel harassed in that nobody enjoys being called a cheater (especially when it is not true); and Eric actually suffered emotional distress in that he missed three days of school. . . .

Facing Other Problems

Without a doubt, the decision to criminally prosecute a teen is not an easy one to make. As elected officials, many prosecutors experience intense pressure from their constituents. In the cyberbullying context, for example, the prosecutor may be riddled with requests from parents of teen victims demanding that another teen be prosecuted for that teen's conduct online. Choosing to prosecute a young adult for this type of conduct has serious potential consequences on the future of that person and raises the question of whether there is a better alternative.

While it remains to be seen whether there is a better choice, alternatives clearly exist as do alternative consequences. Teens can be suspended or expelled from school. Schools might use criminal laws similar to those discussed in this article as a basis for choosing to suspend or expel. In the light of the role of schools as temporary guardians of kids, it would not be surprising if schools act aggressively in addressing perceived wrongs by students. Teens could be denied admission to a school. They could be denied a job. Teens and their parents could be sued. In all instances, a violation of one of the criminal laws could strongly support the unfortunate consequence. Teens can get in trouble even if their own fingers are not on the keys; merely supporting the person behind the keyboard might be enough to cause problems for the teen.

People are looking at what our teens are doing online: a victim's parent contemplating a lawsuit, a school considering expulsion, law enforcement looking to force a change in behavior, or a sexual predator or fraudster looking for an easy victim. Teens need to know or be reminded that there are consequences to choices made online. It is best to assume that no digital communication is ever private. One's words can be used in a variety of unintended ways.

We all play a role in making the Internet and high-tech devices safe for our kids and young adults: teens, parents, educators, law enforcement, and the general public. All need to be aware of the happenings in the online world and the potential legal consequences of offensive, inappropriate or illegal conduct online. More information and greater awareness will, hopefully, lead to more responsible usage of the many high-tech devices available today and a safer online world for our teens.

Notes

1. "Teens Reveal Too Much Online." www.wirednews.com.
2. Ben Schmitt, "Man held in teen's Web seduction," May 16, 2006. www.freep.com.
3. "Teens arrested after posting alleged firebombing video on MySpace.com." www.usatoday.com.
4. Christy Arboscello et al., "Girl, 12, Charged As Sender Of Threat: Terrorism law used; Chippewa Valley kids just glad it's over," December 16, 2005. www.freep.com.
5. Greg Frost, "Harvard Snubs 119 Cyber-Snoop Applicants," March 8, 2005.
6. Martha Irvine, "Too much? Some employers check blogs, posts for data on applicants," January 2, 2007. www.lansingstatejournal.com.
7. Anne Broache, "Principal sues ex-students over MySpace profiles," http://news.cnet.com.
8. "Juvenile Crime," June 26, 2005. www.freep.com.
9. Ross Romaniuk, "Posed as teacher? Police charge 15-year-old alleged Facebook faker." winnipegsun.com.

> "School officials must ensure a secure
> learning environment—and foster one
> that respects student rights."

Teens' First Amendment Rights Must Be Balanced with Their Safety

David L. Hudson Jr.

In the following viewpoint, David L. Hudson Jr. describes reactions that many school administrators had after two students at Columbine High School in Littleton, Colorado, shot and killed several classmates and themselves at the school in 1999. According to Hudson, many people believed that school officials should have recognized the danger the two troubled shooters posed. Administrators responded to these accusations by restricting student speech and becoming overly alarmed when students created violent expressive materials, such as images or writing on a website. School safety is an important concern, he argues, but officials must also be careful not to interfere with students' rights to freedom of expression. Hudson, a research attorney at the First Amendment Center at Vanderbilt University, has written several books, including The Silencing of Student Voices: Preserving Free Speech in America's

Schools *(2003) and* Let the Students Speak!: A History of the Fight for Free Expression in American Schools *(2011).*

L ittleton, Colo., Pearl, Miss., Springfield, Ore., Fayetteville, Tenn., Jonesboro, Ark., and Red Lake, Minn. School shootings in these cities have seared the souls of our collective conscience, making us recoil in horror. The questions naturally come to us: How could this happen? What can school officials do to ensure this doesn't happen again?

Dylan Klebold and Eric Harris—the Columbine High School students-turned-mass murderers—may have signaled in their writings their propensity for violence. Klebold wrote for an English teacher a story so chilling that she showed it to a school counselor and called in the student's parents for a conference. She termed Klebold's story "cruel and disturbing." Harris operated a Web site that contained numerous rants about violence and mayhem. His site said such things as, "God, I can't wait until I can kill you people." Neighbors complained to police that Harris had threatened their son on the Internet. Klebold and Harris made a video titled "Hitman for Hire" at Columbine for a school project.

Students from Columbine High School watch as classmates are evacuated. School administrators have become more worried about violent speech since the shooting in 1999. © Mark Leffingwell/AFP/Getty Images.

Ken Trump, president of the National School Safety and Security Services, said teachers and administrators should pay close attention to such warning signs. "Art teachers and English teachers are often in the best position to recognize early warning signs of potential violence as students who are troubled may communicate these 'red flags' in their drawings and writings," he said. "School officials should be alert to such communications and treat them seriously—meaning that they investigate further with an emphasis on providing support to students determined to be legitimately troubled prior to an incident occurring. Some initial concerns may turn out to be unfounded, but this cannot be determined if the initial signs are overlooked or dismissed."

A Widespread Crackdown

In this post-Columbine world, some school administrators have reacted swiftly to student expression that contains harsh language, violent themes or similar content. In the age of Columbine, zero tolerance has spread from drugs and weapons to controversial student speech. Students have been punished for dark poetry, rap songs, Halloween essays, doodles of teachers and students with sticks in their heads and other material. In some cases, intervention was necessary, justified or wise. At other times, the fear for safety has led to the suppression of constitutional rights. "There's no question that we have seen a widespread crackdown on student expression in the post-Columbine period," said First Amendment lawyer Kevin O'Shea.

School officials have a primary duty to ensure a safe learning environment. Students cannot learn if they fear for their safety. Given incidents such as Columbine, shouldn't school administrators pay close attention to any student expression deemed violent or unusual? "Courts must keep in mind that given Columbine, we must give school professionals the benefit of the doubt," said Thomas Hutton, staff attorney with the National School Board Association.

But the Columbine situation has led to some overreactions. Students have been suspended, expelled, sent to psychologists, even jailed. In some instances, particularly when a student has a history of violent conduct, the punishment may appear sound. But in other cases such judgments appear less so. A middle-school student in Texas spent several days in jail for a Halloween essay for which he received an "A" from his teacher. An honors student in Kansas was expelled for writing a poem about seeking revenge against someone for killing her dog. A student in Louisiana with no history of violence was punished for a 2-year-old drawing he created at home that showed his school under attack.

"Of course there are overreactions," Hutton said. "But that is the exception, the rarity. Sometimes it is only after the fact that it is clearly shown that the school response was an overreaction."

When school officials punish students for their expressive materials, their writings and speech, the question becomes whether they are violating the First Amendment to the U.S. Constitution. The First Amendment protects expressive material. Poems, essays, diaries and writings on a Web site qualify as expression within the meaning of the First Amendment.

The quandary facing school officials is how to balance school safety with the duty to ensure the protection of students' constitutional rights. "Unfortunately, there exists no clear calculus or formula for balancing these important and maybe conflicting duties," said Todd DeMitchell, an education professor at the University of New Hampshire.

Some argue that school officials are in the best position to gauge how to deal with controversial student expression. Others question the policy of silencing any student speech deemed controversial, arguing that silencing students can breed greater alienation and resentment. First Amendment Center Senior Scholar Charles Haynes has written: "In this pressure-cooker, post-Columbine era, more and more schools are taking the path of least resistance: Clamp down on student expression, police the hall and avoid controversy and conflict at all costs." . . .

Balancing Safety and First Amendment Rights

Educators face a difficult challenge as they try to balance school safety with the need to protect students' constitutional rights. At times, it appears the two goals conflict with one another. However, ACLU of Washington staff attorney Aaron Caplan said the apparent conflict is a "false dichotomy"—that school officials can do both.

Interviews with several experts revealed a variety of recommendations for school officials.

School officials should consider a range of factors and options when dealing with violent-themed student expression. Every student is different. Most students who create forms of violent expression will not act out in a rampage like Klebold and Harris. School officials should evaluate the relevant facts and consider context before deciding on a course of action. There are many factors for school officials to consider before initiating their planned response. These include evaluating the student's disciplinary history, relationship with fellow students and teachers, home life, the impact on the specific target of a perceived threat, if applicable, and the reasons the student communicated the violent sentiment if reasonably ascertainable. . . .

In many cases safety should trump freedom of speech. School officials would be negligent if they didn't examine students' violent expression. "All teachers, administrators and school support staff should be attentive to potential warning signs of threatening behavior," said school-safety expert Ken Trump.

Caplan conceded that "schools do not have to ignore danger signs." He said that if a teacher or school counselor has reason to know that a student is troubled or dangerous, the school official should look into the matter.

"In tough situations, there is no formulaic approach," said National School Board Association staff attorney Thomas Hutton. "These are professional judgment calls." He said that the

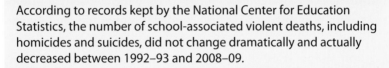

ARE SCHOOLS BECOMING MORE DANGEROUS?

According to records kept by the National Center for Education Statistics, the number of school-associated violent deaths, including homicides and suicides, did not change dramatically and actually decreased between 1992–93 and 2008–09.

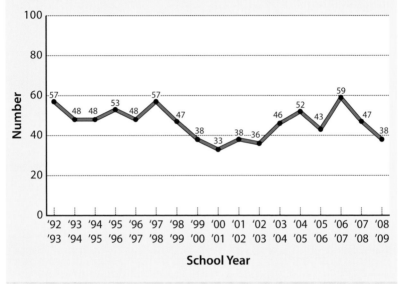

Taken from: Amanda Lenhart, Kristen Purcell, Aaron Smith, and Kathryn Zickhur, "Social Media and Young Adults," Pew Internet and American Life Project, February 3, 2010.

school's approach has to be "contextual": School officials have to consider many different factors. These, he said, should include other indicators and risk factors such as whether the student has been the target of bullies or has a difficult home life. . . .

Day to day, schools must operate in a manner that respects student rights as officials strive to provide a safe environment. School officials must ensure a secure learning environment—and foster one that respects student rights. [Former teacher, principal and superintendent Todd] DeMitchell explained: "For me there are two core concepts that ground my decision making—I must take reasonable steps to keep my students safe, and I must provide an environment in which students are treated with the dignity and respect they deserve." . . .

The question remains what school officials can do to serve both goals—ensuring safety and protecting freedom of expression. O'Shea said, "The two goals are entirely consistent."

"School officials need to learn all they can about the First Amendment and attendant legal requirements, however, before they decide how to balance safety and expression," O'Shea added. "It takes a little more work, but in the long run it will save the schools (and students) a lot of unnecessary grief."

"The problem we're facing in terms of speech is that it may be true that with students who write or create violent images, there is a really small segment of those students who might commit violence," Caplan said. "Do we then suddenly say 'Use such violent expression as a [predictor] for future dangerousness'?"

Although the Center on Juvenile and Criminal Justice has stated that there is "no magic bullet for school safety," creating "an atmosphere of nonviolence is crucial to making schools safer." School safety "cannot be achieved by compromising the constitutional guarantees" of students.

> "The Constitution does not guarantee
> that any person has unlimited access to
> anything."

The Communications Decency Act Protects Children Without Restricting Adult Communication

J. James Exon

In the following viewpoint, Senator J. James Exon of Nebraska defends his proposed bill, the Communications Decency Act, against charges that it will violate the First Amendment of the Constitution. The law requires Internet pornography providers to keep their material away from minors, he explains, and gives law enforcement officials new tools to prosecute those who harm children with online pornography or who approach them online for sexual contact. The Constitutional rights of adults will be protected, he concludes, but those rights are not unlimited. Exon proposed his bill in 1995, and it became law in 1996. In a unanimous decision in 1997, the US Supreme Court ruled that the indecency provisions of the law violated the First Amendment.

J. James Exon, "Some Groups Will Do Anything to Defend the Status Quo on the Internet," *Windows Magazine*, vol. 6, no. 11, October 1995, p. 81+. Copyrighted 2012.

Some groups will do anything to defend the status quo on the Internet. These same people know no bounds when it comes to propagating misinformation about the Communications Decency Act.

Time, Newsweek, USA Today, NBC News and other reputable sources have substantiated the avalanche of obscenity and indecency available to children on the Internet. It's not simply nude pictures or "cheesecake," but the most depraved, lewd material imaginable, from pedophilia to bestiality.

If an individual in your neighborhood were distributing pornographic material to children, or if someone were posting lewd photographs on lampposts and telephone poles, the public would be outraged. I suspect and hope most people would call the police to arrest and charge the person responsible.

These very offenses are occurring every day in America's electronic neighborhoods. If it's not right to permit this activity in the streets of our communities, it's not right to ignore it when it's happening in our homes, schools and libraries via a computer screen.

Free Access Creates Problems

Nor is it right to allow those who distribute pornography for profit to have access to children. These groups offer free access to pornographic material they normally charge for as a teaser to gain subscribers to their paid services. It's illegal to transmit obscene material such as this through the mail or over the telephone, so there's no valid reason to allow it unimpeded on the Internet.

The Communications Decency Act addresses this problem by restricting indecent communications to areas inaccessible to children. Nothing in the legislation applies to constitutionally protected speech between consenting adults. We've addressed the constitutional questions by incorporating court-tested concepts for similar telephone and mail infractions.

(Editor's note: At press time [1995], the House and Senate versions of the Communications Decency Act did not agree. The legislation prohibits transmitting obscene material of any form and indecent material to those under 18. It does not explicitly protect obscene material passed among consenting adults.)

The legislation requires content providers to take reasonable steps to ensure those under 18 can't gain access to this material. It's up to them to decide how to block such access. Some bulletin board systems (BBSes) have already begun by requiring subscribers to provide credit card numbers before they can gain access to certain areas. Such voluntary initiatives are a step in the right direction, but they're not a substitute for well-reasoned law.

An Exciting—and Dangerous— New Era

The Communications Decency Act will give law enforcement the right to prosecute "electronic stalkers," electronic distributors of obscene materials and those who use a computer to make the equivalent of obscene telephone calls. It would also enhance the chances of prosecuting those who provide pornography to children via a computer.

The law won't be foolproof, but it will work. Just like speed limits don't eliminate all speeders on the asphalt highways, they do make the highways safer. We want to set down some basic rules of the road to make the information highway safer for families and children to travel.

Parents and schools must also stay involved to make the Internet safer. Wringing one's hands in dismay and disgust while refusing to do anything to protect children is irresponsible. Parents should make sure they know what sort of services they're subscribing to, supervise their children and prevent them from gaining access to areas they shouldn't be seeing.

Enough of the self-serving philosophy of the "hands-off elite." They seem convinced the framers of the Constitution plotted to ensure the freedom of the profiteering pornographer, the pervert and the pedophile to practice in the presence of children

Vice President Al Gore watches as President Clinton signs the Telecommunications Reform Act, which included the Communications Decency Act, in 1996 at the Library of Congress in Washington, DC. © AP Images/Ron Edmonds.

on a taxpayer-created and subsidized computer network. That's nonsense.

Opponents forsake reason when they maintain that although they want to protect children from indecency, seduction and harassment, the overriding issue is freedom of access to anything by anybody. Tell that to a parent whose child was lured away by a deviate on a computer network.

We're in the infancy of an exciting new era. The information highway is certain to be the greatest boon to information dissemination since the printing press. We should reason together to address the serious and well-documented problems with this technology.

The Communications Decency Act targets those who use the Internet to offer pornography to children while at the same time protecting the Constitutional rights of adults. The Act seeks

"You don't need to tell me about the birds and the bees. I downloaded it all from the Internet," Aaron Bacall. CartoonStock.com.

to isolate indecent communications, requiring online services to take "reasonable" measures to prevent those under the age of 18 from accessing the material. A few bulletin boards services voluntarily ask for credit card numbers before allowing access to restricted areas, but a comprehensive, well-thought-out law is required. The Act simply gives law officers the ability to prosecute those who use electronic methods to distribute obscene materials. All responsibility does not rest with the law, of course, and schools and parents must monitor their children's computer use as well as the types of services to which the family subscribes. The Constitution does not guarantee that any person has unlimited access to anything.

> *"The governmental interest in protecting children from harmful materials . . . does not justify an unnecessarily broad suppression of speech addressed to adults."*

Limitations on 'Patently Offensive Display' Violate the First Amendment

The Supreme Court's Decision

John Paul Stevens

The following viewpoint is taken from the majority opinion in the 1997 US Supreme Court case Reno v. American Civil Liberties Union, *written by Justice John Paul Stevens. The case concerned the Communications Decency Act of 1996 (CDA), the first attempt by the US Congress to regulate Internet pornography. The Act, which made it illegal to "knowingly" make "obscene or indecent" material available to anyone under the age of eighteen, was challenged by the American Civil Liberties Union (ACLU) and other groups, and defended in court by US Attorney General Janet Reno. In his opinion, Stevens agrees with the ACLU that the terms "obscene" and "indecent" are too vague, it is difficult for Internet content providers to guarantee that children will not access their sites, and it is unconstitutional to keep legal materials—including*

John Paul Stevens, Majority Opinion, *Reno v. American Civil Liberties Union*, US Supreme Court, June 26, 1997.

pornography—away from adults in order to keep children from having access to them. Stevens served on the Supreme Court from 1975 to 2010.

A t issue is the constitutionality of two statutory provisions enacted to protect minors from "indecent" and "patently offensive" communications on the Internet. Notwithstanding the legitimacy and importance of the congressional goal of protecting children from harmful materials, we agree with the three judge District Court that the statute abridges "the freedom of speech" protected by the First Amendment. . . .

Sexually Explicit Material

Sexually explicit material on the Internet includes text, pictures, and chat and "extends from the modestly titillating to the hardest core." These files are created, named, and posted in the same manner as material that is not sexually explicit, and may be accessed either deliberately or unintentionally during the course of an imprecise search. . . .

Though such material is widely available, users seldom encounter such content accidentally. "A document's title or a description of the document will usually appear before the document itself . . . and in many cases the user will receive detailed information about a site's content before he or she need take the step to access the document. Almost all sexually explicit images are preceded by warnings as to the content." For that reason, the "odds are slim" that a user would enter a sexually explicit site by accident. Unlike communications received by radio or television, "the receipt of information on the Internet requires a series of affirmative steps more deliberate and directed than merely turning a dial. A child requires some sophistication and some ability to read to retrieve material and thereby to use the Internet unattended."

Systems have been developed to help parents control the material that may be available on a home computer with Internet

ACLU senior staff counsel Chris Hansen (left) holds a news conference in Philadelphia on February 8, 1996, to discuss a lawsuit against the Communications Decency Act. © AP Images/Nanine Hartenbusch.

access. A system may either limit a computer's access to an approved list of sources that have been identified as containing no adult material, it may block designated inappropriate sites, or it may attempt to block messages containing identifiable objectionable features. "Although parental control software currently can screen for certain suggestive words or for known sexually explicit sites, it cannot now screen for sexually explicit images." Nevertheless, the evidence indicates that "a reasonably effective method by which parents can prevent their children from accessing sexually explicit and other material which parents may believe is inappropriate for their children will soon be available."

Age Verification

The problem of age verification differs for different uses of the Internet. The District Court categorically determined that there "is no effective way to determine the identity or the age of a user who is accessing material through e-mail, mail exploders, newsgroups or chat rooms." The Government offered no evidence that there was a reliable way to screen recipients and participants in such fora for age. Moreover, even if it were technologically feasible to block minors' access to newsgroups and chat rooms containing discussions of art, politics or other subjects that potentially elicit "indecent" or "patently offensive" contributions, it would not be possible to block their access to that material and "still allow them access to the remaining content, even if the overwhelming majority of that content was not indecent."

Technology exists by which an operator of a Web site may condition access on the verification of requested information such as a credit card number or an adult password. Credit card verification is only feasible, however, either in connection with a commercial transaction in which the card is used, or by payment to a verification agency. Using credit card possession as a surrogate for proof of age would impose costs on non commercial Web sites that would require many of them to shut down. For that reason, at the time of the trial, credit card verification was "effectively unavailable to a substantial number of Internet content providers." Moreover, the imposition of such a requirement "would completely bar adults who do not have a credit card and lack the resources to obtain one from accessing any blocked material." . . .

Two Questionable Provisions

The Telecommunications Act of 1996 was an unusually important legislative enactment. . . . Title V [part of the Act]—known as the "Communications Decency Act of 1996" (CDA)—contains the two statutory provisions challenged in this case. They are informally described as the "indecent transmission" provision and the "patently offensive display" provision.

The first prohibits the knowing transmission of obscene or indecent messages to any recipient under 18 years of age. . . .

The second provision prohibits the knowing sending or displaying of patently offensive messages in a manner that is available to a person under 18 years of age. . . .

On February 8, 1996, immediately after the President signed the statute, 20 plaintiffs filed suit against the Attorney General of the United States and the Department of Justice challenging the constitutionality of [these provisions]. A week later, based on his conclusion that the term "indecent" was too vague to provide the basis for a criminal prosecution, District Judge Buckwalter entered a temporary restraining order against enforcement insofar as it applies to indecent communications. A second suit was then filed by 27 additional plaintiffs, the two cases were consolidated, and a three judge District Court was convened. . . . Each of the three judges wrote a separate opinion, but their judgment was unanimous. . . .

Judge Buckwalter concluded that the word "indecent" and the terms "patently offensive" and "in context" were so vague that criminal enforcement of either section would violate the "fundamental constitutional principle" of "simple fairness," and the specific protections of the First and Fifth Amendments. He found no statutory basis for the Government's argument that the challenged provisions would be applied only to "pornographic" materials, noting that, unlike obscenity, "indecency has *not* been defined to exclude works of serious literary, artistic, political or scientific value." Moreover, the Government's claim that the work must be considered patently offensive "in context" was itself vague because the relevant context might "refer to, among other things, the nature of the communication as a whole, the time of day it was conveyed, the medium used, the identity of the speaker, or whether or not it is accompanied by appropriate warnings." He believed that the unique nature of the Internet aggravated the vagueness of the statute. . . .

According to data from Reporters Without Borders and the OpenNet Initiative, most countries that are connected to the Internet conduct some level of Internet censorship. The United States practices "some censorship," according to the data.

Taken from: Yuxi Yu, "So You Think the Internet Is Free," 2011. open.yuxiyou.net.

The Government appealed [the ruling]. In its appeal, the Government argues that the District Court erred in holding that the CDA violated both the First Amendment because it is overbroad and the Fifth Amendment because it is vague. While

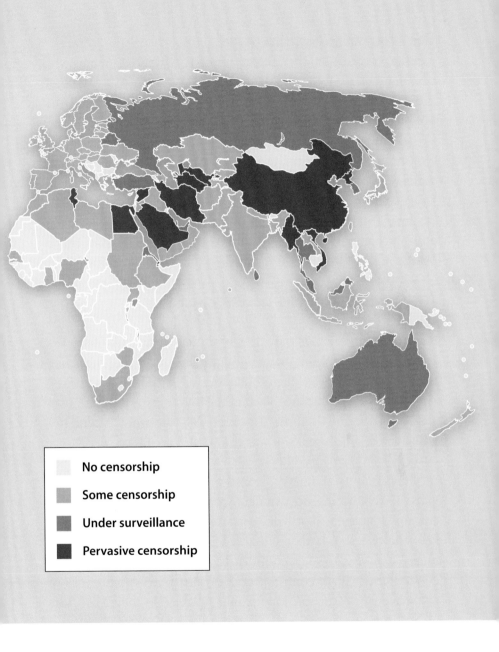

No censorship

Some censorship

Under surveillance

Pervasive censorship

we discuss the vagueness of the CDA because of its relevance to the First Amendment overbreadth inquiry, we conclude that the judgment should be affirmed without reaching the Fifth Amendment issue. . . .

The Internet Is Not 'Invasive'

Neither before nor after the enactment of the CDA have the vast democratic fora of the Internet been subject to the type of government supervision and regulation that has attended the broadcast industry. Moreover, the Internet is not as "invasive" as radio or television. The District Court specifically found that "[c]ommunications over the Internet do not 'invade' an individual's home or appear on one's computer screen unbidden. Users seldom encounter content 'by accident.'" It also found that "[a]lmost all sexually explicit images are preceded by warnings as to the content," and cited testimony that "'odds are slim' that a user would come across a sexually explicit sight by accident." . . .

The Communications Decency Act Lacks Precision

Regardless of whether the CDA is so vague that it violates the Fifth Amendment, the many ambiguities concerning the scope of its coverage render it problematic for purposes of the First Amendment. For instance, each of the two parts of the CDA uses a different linguistic form. The first uses the word "indecent," while the second speaks of material that "in context, depicts or describes, in terms patently offensive as measured by contemporary community standards, sexual or excretory activities or organs." Given the absence of a definition of either term, this difference in language will provoke uncertainty among speakers about how the two standards relate to each other and just what they mean. Could a speaker confidently assume that a serious discussion about birth control practices, homosexuality . . . or the consequences of prison rape would not violate the CDA? This uncertainty undermines the likelihood that the CDA has been carefully tailored to the congressional goal of protecting minors from potentially harmful materials. . . .

We are persuaded that the CDA lacks the precision that the First Amendment requires when a statute regulates the content of speech. In order to deny minors access to potentially harmful speech, the CDA effectively suppresses a large amount of speech that adults have a constitutional right to receive and to address to one another. That burden on adult speech is unacceptable if less restrictive alternatives would be at least as effective in achieving the legitimate purpose that the statute was enacted to serve.

In evaluating the free speech rights of adults, we have made it perfectly clear that "[s]exual expression which is indecent but not obscene is protected by the First Amendment."

It is true that we have repeatedly recognized the governmental interest in protecting children from harmful materials. But that interest does not justify an unnecessarily broad suppression of speech addressed to adults. As we have explained, the Government may not "reduc[e] the adult population . . . to . . . only what is fit for children." "[R]egardless of the strength of the government's interest" in protecting children, "[t]he level of discourse reaching a mailbox simply cannot be limited to that which would be suitable for a sandbox." . . .

The record demonstrates that the growth of the Internet has been and continues to be phenomenal. As a matter of constitutional tradition, in the absence of evidence to the contrary, we presume that governmental regulation of the content of speech is more likely to interfere with the free exchange of ideas than to encourage it. The interest in encouraging freedom of expression in a democratic society outweighs any theoretical but unproven benefit of censorship.

| "There is a crucial distinction between providing minors with harmful matter . . . and maintaining computers where minors may obtain such matter, however easily."

Public Libraries Cannot Be Required to Prevent Children from Seeing Online Pornography

The State Appeal Court's Decision

Court of Appeal of the State of California

The following viewpoint is taken from a 2001 decision by a Court of Appeal in California. The case was filed by the mother of a then twelve-year-old boy (referred to in the viewpoint as the "appellant"), who charges that the public library in her hometown, Livermore, California (the "respondent"), should have taken more steps to prevent her son from downloading pornography from library computers. The mother, Kathleen R., sued the city in Superior Court, lost, and filed an appeal. In its decision, the Court of Appeal found that the library had informed patrons that computers were available and unrestricted and had been clear about its position that it was the responsibility of parents—not of the library—to make decisions about what minors should see on the Internet. Even though it is

Kathleen R. v. City of Livermore, Court of Appeal of the State of California, First Appellate District, Division Four, March 6, 2001.

easy to find pornography and other controversial material on the Internet, the Court concluded, making computers available is not the same thing as providing those materials. The Court agreed with the earlier decision, finding in favor of the city.

I n this case we hold that a city is not subject to suit for damages or an injunction for offering unrestricted access to the Internet through computers at a public library.

This case was filed against respondent City of Livermore [California] by appellant Kathleen R. individually, and in her capacities as a taxpayer and as guardian *ad litem* [for the suit] for Brandon P., her minor son. . . .

Unsupervised Access

Respondent's library has computers linked to the Internet which patrons of any age are free to use. Twelve-year-old Brandon went to the computers without appellant's knowledge and downloaded sexually explicit photos from the Internet onto a floppy disk that he brought to the library. Without any adult's knowledge or permission Brandon printed the photos at a relative's computer. He engaged in this activity on about 10 occasions. Appellant alleges that the photos Brandon obtained are harmful to minors and that some of them are obscene. One of the photos is reproduced in color on the first page of the complaint and others are attached as exhibits. In one of the exhibits a middle school schedule is superimposed over the image of a scantily clad woman. Brandon showed the photos to other minors.

A copy of the Internet access policy adopted by respondent's library board of trustees is attached to the complaint. This policy states in part: "The Board of Trustees supports the idea that all members of the community have free and equal access to the entire range of library resources, regardless of content, approach, format or amount of detail. These rights extend to all users of the public library including minors. . . . The Internet and its available resources may contain materials of a controversial nature. The

No Age Verification

You can be any age you want to be online. Kids can pretend they are adults and adults can pretend they are kids. And it's easy. How is that possible? Anyone asking you to verify or confirm your age simply takes your word for it. There's no verification. The prevailing attitude of sites that ask your age is that they don't really care how old you are. If they state that you must be 21 to enter their site, or if they just ask you to enter your birth date on an application form, they've done their job. The law only requires sites to ask a user's age and they are in the clear, even on kid sites. It may be wrong, but it's the law. And if you wonder why they don't verify, follow the money. The internet is big business and there is lots of money that can be made from kids online. There are two sides to this age problem. The more obvious problem is that kids can lie about their age to gain access to sites that are adult-oriented or that offer access to age-restricted items like drugs, alcohol, or gambling. Conversely, adults can pretend they're kids and make their way into chat groups and social networking sites. And that's exactly what sexual predators do.

Vincent J. Schiavone, Bob Kessinger, John Sancin, and Barb Rose, Surfing Among the Cyber Sharks. *Prioratus Press, 2009, pp. 25–26. www.cyberpatrol.com.*

Livermore Public Library does not monitor and has no control over the information accessed through the Internet and cannot be held responsible for its content. . . . Library patrons use the Internet at their own risk. . . . Individuals must accept responsibility for determining what is appropriate. The Library . . . upholds and affirms the right of each individual to have access to constitutionally protected materials and also affirms the right and responsibility of parents to determine and monitor their children's use of library materials and resources. Parents and guardians are encouraged to work closely with their children. Parents are expected to monitor and supervise children's use of the Internet in selecting material that is consistent with personal and family values. The Livermore Public Library does not provide this monitoring or supervision." The policy lists examples of "unacceptable use" of computers, including use "for other than educational, informational and recreational purposes," or for "unauthorized, illegal or unethical purposes."

In her state law claims, appellant alleges that: Respondent is wasting public funds on computers which provide access to obscenity and matter harmful to minors; it is a public nuisance for respondent to knowingly allow its computers to be used to access obscenity and matter harmful to minors; and the library is unsafe for minors because the computers provide them with access to harmful matter. The claim alleges that: Minors are expected to go to the library to complete public school assignments; the library encourages minors to use its computers; the library has a policy of allowing minors to view and download obscenity and pornography on the computers; minors exposed to obscenity and pornography suffer emotional and psychological damage and damage to their nervous systems; respondent knows its actions and policies are placing minors at grave risk of harm; and respondent tries to keep parents ignorant of that risk. . . .

Are Libraries Providing Pornography?

A public library is in a "damned if you do, damned if you don't" situation in deciding whether to restrict access to the Internet from its computers to prevent harm to minors. A case in Virginia shows that the library can be sued if it limits Internet access (*Mainstream Loudoun v. Bd. of Trustees of Loudoun* [use of filtering software violated First Amendment]); this case shows that the library can be sued if it does not. . . .

At various points in her arguments, appellant suggests that respondent can be held liable for providing obscene pornography to minors, even if librarians themselves do not actually

A decision in 2001 by the Court of Appeal of the State of California ruled that public libraries were not required to filter Internet content. © ColorBlind Images/Iconica/Getty Images.

exhibit such matter to minors or teach them how to access it, merely because of the ease with which such images can be obtained from the Internet. In *Reno v. American Civil Liberties Union*, the court recognized that "[s]exually explicit material on the Internet includes text, pictures, and chat and 'extends from the modestly titillating to the hardest-core.' . . . [It] may be accessed either deliberately or unintentionally during the course of an imprecise search." However, the court found that "users seldom encounter such content accidentally. . . . 'Almost all sexually explicit images are preceded by warnings as to content.' For that reason, the 'odds are slim' that a user would enter a sexually explicit site by accident." Here, it is not alleged that Brandon stumbled across anything harmful by accident. Nevertheless, appellant has likened library computers to "a machine where you push a red button, [and] obscene pornography appears on the screen." Appellant's briefs represent that "an impressionable child need only type the word 'girl' [into a library computer] and click thrice to view obscene perversions of the darkest order." Appellant has advised that she has experts who can demonstrate "it's so easy to obtain obscene pornography from library terminals in the City of Livermore that's basically the same thing as City librarians simply providing pornography." Thus, appellant argues that respondent has a "policy of essentially giving obscene pornography to any willing child who asks."

Contrary to this line of argument, there is a crucial distinction between providing minors with harmful matter on the one hand and maintaining computers where minors may obtain such matter, however easily, on the other. . . .

Patrons Use the Internet 'at Their Own Risk'

A library does not "affirmatively plac[e]" minors in danger by allowing them unsupervised use of computers which are linked to the Internet. . . . The library's Internet policy did not compel minors to use the library's computers, or create any of the harmful matter accessible through such use. . . .

As previously noted, appellant's briefs assert that the library has a policy of providing obscene pornography to minors. Appellant contends that the policy, as so conceived, violates minors' "liberty interest in personal security and freedom from restraint and infliction of pain." Appellant submits that minors are seriously injured by viewing obscene pornography, that freedom from infliction of such pain is a fundamental constitutional right which cannot be infringed without a compelling state interest, and that there is no such interest here because "there is no 'compelling' reason to give children any access to the Internet at all." In the same vein, appellant's briefs assert that respondent's librarians are giving minors obscene pornography, and thus that this case concerns harm inflicted by government employees, rather than their mere failure to provide protection.

These arguments are insupportable because it is not the policy of respondent's library to provide minors with obscene pornography. Provision of computer-transmitted obscenity to minors would contravene the library policy's directives that computers be used for educational, informational, recreational, but not illegal, purposes. The policy warns that "controversial" material is available on the Internet, that patrons who use the Internet do so "at their own risk," and that the library does not supervise minors' use of the Internet. This acknowledgement that the library does not undertake to protect minors from harmful matter on the Internet does not imply that the library intends for minors to be exposed to obscenity. The library's affirmation of "the right of each individual to have access to constitutionally protected materials" is not an endorsement of minors' access to obscenity.

> *"Congress has wide latitude to attach conditions to the receipt of federal assistance in order to further its policy objectives."*

Requiring Internet Filters at Public Libraries Does Not Violate the First Amendment

The Supreme Court's Decision

William H. Rehnquist

In the following viewpoint, US Supreme Court Chief Justice William H. Rehnquist writes for a plurality of justices in explaining why the Court ruled in 2003 that public libraries with Internet services paid for by the federal government could be required to install filtering software to prevent minors from looking at pornography on the Internet. Groups, including the American Library Association, argued that these filters put libraries in the position of violating the First Amendment rights of library patrons to make their own choices about what to look at, and the District Court agreed; in reversing the District Court's ruling, the Supreme Court argued that public libraries are not required to offer every conceivable type of material, and that Congress had the authority to limit

William H. Rehnquist, Plurality opinion, *United States v. American Library Association*, US Supreme Court, June 23, 2003.

how its money is spent. Rehnquist served on the Supreme Court from 1972 to 2005 and became Chief Justice in 1986.

To address the problems associated with the availability of Internet pornography in public libraries, Congress enacted the Children's Internet Protection Act (CIPA) [in 2002]. Under CIPA, a public library may not receive federal assistance to provide Internet access unless it installs software to block images that constitute obscenity or child pornography, and to prevent minors from obtaining access to material that is harmful to them. The District Court held these provisions facially invalid on the ground that they induce public libraries to violate patrons' First Amendment rights. We now reverse.

To help public libraries provide their patrons with Internet access, Congress offers two forms of federal assistance. First, the E-rate program established by the Telecommunications Act of 1996 entitles qualifying libraries to buy Internet access at a discount. In the year ending June 30, 2002, libraries received $58.5 million in such discounts. Second, pursuant to the Library Services and Technology Act (LSTA), the Institute of Museum and Library Services makes grants to state library administrative agencies to "electronically lin[k] libraries with educational, social, or information services," "assis[t] libraries in accessing information through electronic networks," and "pa[y] costs for libraries to acquire or share computer systems and telecommunications technologies." In fiscal year 2002, Congress appropriated more than $149 million in LSTA grants. These programs have succeeded greatly in bringing Internet access to public libraries: By 2000, 95% of the Nation's libraries provided public Internet access.

Problems with Pornography

By connecting to the Internet, public libraries provide patrons with a vast amount of valuable information. But there is also an enormous amount of pornography on the Internet, much of

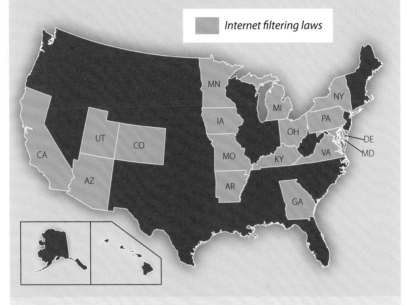

STATE FILTERING LAWS

Supplementing federal laws, seventeen states have their own Internet filtering laws that require public libraries to adopt Internet use policies to prevent minors from gaining access to sexually explicit, obscene or harmful materials.

Internet filtering laws

Taken from: National Conference of State Legislatures, "Children and the Internet: Laws Relating to Filtering, Blocking and Usage Policies in Schools and Libraries," January 13, 2011.

which is easily obtained. The accessibility of this material has created serious problems for libraries, which have found that patrons of all ages, including minors, regularly search for on-line pornography. Some patrons also expose others to pornographic images by leaving them displayed on Internet terminals or printed at library printers.

Upon discovering these problems, Congress became concerned that the E-rate and LSTA programs were facilitating access to illegal and harmful pornography. Congress learned that adults "us[e] library computers to access pornography that is then exposed to staff, passersby, and children," and that "minors acces[s] child and adult pornography in libraries."

But Congress also learned that filtering software that blocks access to pornographic Web sites could provide a reasonably effective way to prevent such uses of library resources. By 2000, before Congress enacted CIPA, almost 17% of public libraries used such software on at least some of their Internet terminals, and 7% had filters on all of them. A library can set such software to block categories of material, such as "Pornography" or "Violence." When a patron tries to view a site that falls within such a category, a screen appears indicating that the site is blocked. But a filter set to block pornography may sometimes block other sites that present neither obscene nor pornographic material, but that nevertheless trigger the filter. To minimize this problem, a library can set its software to prevent the blocking of material that falls into categories like "Education," "History," and "Medical." A library may also add or delete specific sites from a blocking category, and anyone can ask companies that furnish filtering software to unblock particular sites.

Responding to this information, Congress enacted CIPA. It provides that a library may not receive E-rate or LSTA assistance unless it has "a policy of Internet safety for minors that includes the operation of a technology protection measure . . . that protects against access" by all persons to "visual depictions" that constitute "obscen[ity]" or "child pornography," and that protects against access by minors to "visual depictions" that are "harmful to minors." The statute defines a "[t]echnology protection measure" as "a specific technology that blocks or filters Internet access to material covered by" CIPA. CIPA also permits the library to "disable" the filter "to enable access for bona fide research or other lawful purposes." Under the E-rate program, disabling is permitted "during use by an adult." Under the LSTA program, disabling is permitted during use by any person.

Appellees are a group of libraries, library associations, library patrons, and Web site publishers, including the American

Part of the US Supreme Court ruling requiring Internet filters at public libraries argues that just as books are carefully reviewed and chosen for their collection so should Internet access. © John Giustina/Iconica/Getty Images.

Library Association (ALA) and the Multnomah County Public Library in Portland, Oregon. They sued the United States and the Government agencies and officials responsible for administering the E-rate and LSTA programs in District Court, challenging the constitutionality of CIPA's filtering provisions. . . .

After a trial, the District Court ruled that CIPA was facially unconstitutional and enjoined the relevant agencies and officials from withholding federal assistance for failure to comply with CIPA. The District Court held that Congress had exceeded its authority under the Spending Clause, U.S. Const., because, in the court's view, "any public library that complies with CIPA's conditions will necessarily violate the First Amendment." . . .

The District Court held that, although the Government has a compelling interest "in preventing the dissemination of obscenity, child pornography, or, in the case of minors, material harmful to minors," the use of software filters is not narrowly tailored to further those interests. We . . . now reverse.

The Role of Libraries

Congress has wide latitude to attach conditions to the receipt of federal assistance in order to further its policy objectives. But Congress may not "induce" the recipient "to engage in activities that would themselves be unconstitutional." To determine whether libraries would violate the First Amendment by employing the filtering software that CIPA requires, we must first examine the role of libraries in our society.

Public libraries pursue the worthy missions of facilitating learning and cultural enrichment. Appellee ALA's Library Bill of Rights states that libraries should provide "[b]ooks and other . . . resources . . . for the interest, information, and enlightenment of all people of the community the library serves." To fulfill their traditional missions, public libraries must have broad discretion to decide what material to provide to their patrons. Although they seek to provide a wide array of information, their goal has never been to provide "universal coverage." Instead, public libraries seek to provide materials "that would be of the greatest direct benefit or interest to the community." To this end, libraries collect only those materials deemed to have "requisite and appropriate quality." . . .

A public library does not acquire Internet terminals in order to create a public forum for Web publishers to express themselves, any more than it collects books in order to provide a public forum for the authors of books to speak. It provides Internet access, not to "encourage a diversity of views from private speakers," but for the same reasons it offers other library resources: to facilitate research, learning, and recreational pursuits by furnishing materials of requisite and appropriate quality. It is "no more than a technological extension of the book stack."

The District Court disagreed because, whereas a library reviews and affirmatively chooses to acquire every book in its collection, it does not review every Web site that it makes available. Based on this distinction, the court reasoned that a public library enjoys less discretion in deciding which Internet materials to make available than in making book selections. We do not find this distinction constitutionally relevant. A library's failure to make quality-based judgments about all the material it furnishes from the Web does not somehow taint the judgments it does make. A library's need to exercise judgment in making collection decisions depends on its traditional role in identifying suitable and worthwhile material; it is no less entitled to play that role when it collects material from the Internet than when it collects material from any other source. Most libraries already exclude pornography from their print collections because they deem it inappropriate for inclusion. We do not subject these decisions to heightened scrutiny; it would make little sense to treat libraries' judgments to block online pornography any differently, when these judgments are made for just the same reason. . . .

The Limitations and Benefits of Filters

Like the District Court, the dissents fault the tendency of filtering software to "overblock"—that is, to erroneously block access to constitutionally protected speech that falls outside the categories that software users intend to block. Due to the software's limitations, "[m]any erroneously blocked [Web] pages contain content that is completely innocuous for both adults and minors, and that no rational person could conclude matches the filtering companies' category definitions, such as 'pornography' or 'sex.'" Assuming that such erroneous blocking presents constitutional difficulties, any such concerns are dispelled by the ease with which patrons may have the filtering software disabled. When a patron encounters a blocked site, he need only ask a librarian to unblock it or (at least in the case of adults) disable the filter. As the District Court found, libraries have the capacity to permanently unblock any erroneously blocked site, and the Solicitor General stated at oral argument that a "library may . . . eliminate the filtering with respect to specific sites . . . at the request of a patron." With respect to adults, CIPA also expressly authorizes library officials to "disable" a filter altogether "to enable access for bona fide research or other lawful purposes." . . .

The E-rate and LSTA programs were intended to help public libraries fulfill their traditional role of obtaining material of requisite and appropriate quality for educational and informational purposes: Congress may certainly insist that these "public funds be spent for the purposes for which they were authorized." Especially because public libraries have traditionally excluded pornographic material from their other collections, Congress could reasonably impose a parallel limitation on its Internet assistance programs. As the use of filtering software helps to carry out these programs, it is a permissible condition. . . .

Because public libraries' use of Internet filtering software does not violate their patrons' First Amendment rights, CIPA does not induce libraries to violate the Constitution, and is a valid exercise of Congress' spending power. Nor does CIPA impose an unconstitutional condition on public libraries. Therefore, the judgment of the District Court for the Eastern District of Pennsylvania is Reversed.

> *"Instead of restricting or denying access to the Internet, librarians and teachers should educate minors to participate responsibly, ethically, and safely."*

Public Libraries Should Not Restrict Minors' Access to the Internet

American Library Association

In the following viewpoint, the American Library Association (ALA) states its position that library patrons under the age of eighteen have the right, under the First Amendment to the US Constitution, to have free access to Internet materials using the computers in public and school libraries. Minors use the Internet for important academic and social purposes, the viewpoint argues. Although some material on the Internet may not be suitable for all children, it concludes, parents and other guardians must take responsibility for monitoring their own children's access; it is wrong to make policies or install filters that limit Internet access more broadly. The viewpoint is an interpretation of part of the ALA's Library Bill of Rights, a document affirming basic policies that, according to the organization, should guide the services offered by all libraries.

The digital environment offers opportunities for accessing, creating, and sharing information. The rights of minors to retrieve, interact with, and create information posted on the Internet in schools and libraries are extensions of their First Amendment rights.

Academic pursuits of minors can be strengthened with the use of interactive Web tools, allowing young people to create documents and share them online; upload pictures, videos, and graphic material; revise public documents; and add tags to online content to classify and organize information. Instances of inappropriate use of such academic tools should be addressed as individual behavior issues, not as justification for restricting or banning access to interactive technology. Schools and libraries should ensure that institutional environments offer opportunities for students to use interactive Web tools constructively in their academic pursuits, as the benefits of shared learning are well documented.

Personal interactions of minors can be enhanced by social tools available through the Internet. Social networking Web sites allow the creation of online communities that feature an open exchange of information in various forms, such as images, videos, blog posts, and discussions about common interests. Interactive Web tools help children and young adults learn about and organize social, civic, and extra-curricular activities. Many interactive sites invite users to establish online identities, share personal information, create Web content, and join social networks. Parents and guardians play a critical role in preparing their children for participation in online activity by communicating their personal family values and by monitoring their children's use of the Internet. Parents and guardians are responsible for what their children—and only their children—access on the Internet in libraries.

Issues of Intellectual Freedom

The use of interactive Web tools poses two competing intellectual freedom issues—the protection of minors' privacy and the

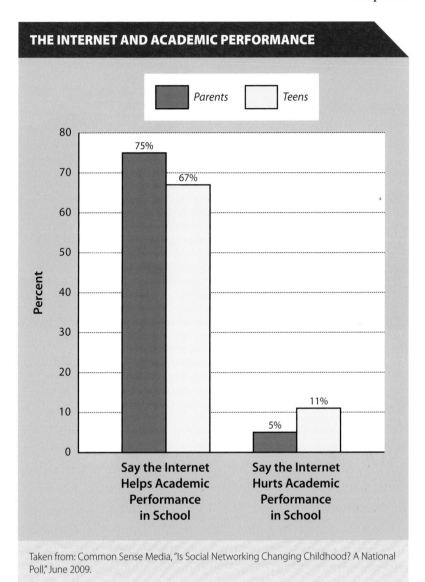

THE INTERNET AND ACADEMIC PERFORMANCE

Parents   Teens

Say the Internet
Helps Academic
Performance
in School

Say the Internet
Hurts Academic
Performance
in School

Taken from: Common Sense Media, "Is Social Networking Changing Childhood? A National Poll," June 2009.

right of free speech. Some have expressed concerns regarding what they perceive is an increased vulnerability of young people in the online environment when they use interactive sites to post personally identifiable information. In an effort to protect minors' privacy, adults sometimes restrict access to interactive

The American Library Association argues that teaching responsible use of computers is more productive than trying to restrict minors' access to the Internet. © Thomas Barwick/The Image Bank/Getty Images.

Web environments. Filters, for example, are sometimes used to restrict access by youth to interactive social networking tools, but at the same time deny minors' rights to free expression on the Internet. Prohibiting children and young adults from using social networking sites does not teach safe behavior and leaves youth without the necessary knowledge and skills to protect their privacy or engage in responsible speech. Instead of restricting or denying access to the Internet, librarians and teachers should educate minors to participate responsibly, ethically, and safely.

The First Amendment applies to speech created by minors on interactive sites. Usage of these social networking sites in a school or library allows minors to access and create resources that fulfill their interests and needs for information, for social connection with peers, and for participation in a community of learners. Restricting expression and access to interactive Web sites because the sites provide tools for sharing information with others violates the tenets of the *Library Bill of Rights*. It is the responsibility of librarians and educators to monitor threats to the intellectual freedom of minors and to advocate for extending access to interactive applications on the Internet.

As defenders of intellectual freedom and the First Amendment, libraries and librarians have a responsibility to offer unrestricted access to Internet interactivity in accordance with local, state, and federal laws and to advocate for greater access where it is abridged. School and library professionals should work closely with young people to help them learn skills and attitudes that will prepare them to be responsible, effective, and productive communicators in a free society.

> "Students need access to information that can accurately and sensitively address their questions, as well as create understanding and tolerance in schools rather than judgment and fear."

A Librarian Discusses Her Efforts to Provide LGBT Resources for Students

Personal Narrative

Karyn Storts-Brinks

In the following viewpoint, high school librarian Karyn Storts-Brinks describes what happened when she and a group of students discovered that their school district's Internet filters blocked websites that gave neutral or positive information about LGBT (lesbian, gay, bisexual and transgender) issues, but did not block sites that were critical of homosexuality. Through the Tennessee chapter of the American Civil Liberties Union (ACLU), the group successfully sued two school districts to remove the filters that prevented students from gaining access to information about sexual orientation. A librarian's job, Storts-Brinks argues, is to provide access to information, and denying students access to these sites is not only a form of illegal censorship but also a withholding of impor-

Karyn Storts-Brinks, "Censorship Online: One School Librarian's Journey to Provide Access to LGBT Resources," *Knowledge Quest*, vol. 39, no. 1, September–October 2010, pp. 22–28.

tant information about health and social well-being. Storts-Brinks, a librarian at Fulton High School in Knoxville, Tennessee, is the recipient of the 2010 Tennessee Library Association Freedom of Information Award and the 2010 American Association of School Libraries Intellectual Freedom Award.

It seems that most school librarians have encountered problems with—and railed against—CIPA [Children's Internet Protection Act]-mandated filters on school computers. My own career has seen a full range of filtering experiences, from no filter at all to an over-filtering situation so egregious that its resolution required an ACLU [American Civil Liberties Union] lawsuit, *Franks v. Metropolitan Board of Public Education*, against the school district that employs me.

The Knox County, Tennessee, school district is vast; it is comprised of fifty elementary schools, fourteen middle schools, and thirteen high schools, as well as other types of schools and centers. As of May 2009, it served 56,516 students of diverse racial and socioeconomic backgrounds. Despite these statistics, Knoxville and its surrounding areas still feel like a quiet hometown community, but the filtering situation that I challenged garnered national media attention before it was all over.

The journey toward resolution began many months before involving civil rights attorneys. In August 2007 I first became aware of websites that seemed inappropriately and unnecessarily blocked by our filtering system, Education Networks of America (ENA). While helping students in the Fulton High School Library with persuasive essays on contemporary topics, I was surprised by our inability to access the sites of both the Human Rights Campaign (HRC) and the Gay Lesbian Straight Education Network (GLSEN). Of note is the fact that GLSEN is an organization that is fully endorsed by the National Education Association (NEA). Among the tools NEA provides on its website is a link to GLSEN and an online guide "Strengthening the Learning Environment: A School Employee's Guide to Gay,

Lesbian, Bisexual, and Transgender Issues" that cites GLSEN's School Climate Survey [and] includes GLSEN among its list of "Additional Resources." . . .

My concern over these blocked websites was underscored by my role as the faculty sponsor of Fulton High's Gay Straight Alliance (GSA). GLSEN's tools and research are unmatched when it comes to providing information and rationale that supports the existence of GSAs in schools. From the powerful statistics gleaned from the National School Climate Survey to the Jump-Start Guide for Gay Straight Alliances, this organization's website offers a wealth of information for students, teachers, and administrators and is intended to improve school success for all students. GLSEN has shown direct correlations between students' ability to achieve, and the presence of GSAs in schools and an overall climate of acceptance.

I submitted my request to ENA to unblock these educational and informative websites. I received a prompt e-mail response from the ENA helpdesk: "We cannot unblock the websites referenced . . . as the site categorization indicates it references/provides access to Sexuality/Alternative Lifestyles." I later discovered that these sites did not meet the criteria for ENA's description of the "Sexuality/Alternative Lifestyles" category. In reviewing the list of blocked categories available through the ENA "blocked website" form, I found one called LGBT: "Sites that provide information regarding, support, promote, or cater to one's sexual orientation or gender identity including but not limited to lesbian, gay, bisexual, and transgender sites. This category does not include sites that are sexually gratuitous in nature which would typically fall under the Pornography category." Thankfully, because of the successful ACLU lawsuit, this LGBT (lesbian, gay, bisexual, and transgender) category is no longer listed, but the reference to these definitions is corroborated in the documentation of the *Franks v. Metropolitan Board of Public Education*.

The results of my efforts to examine the parameters of this blocking were even more disconcerting. Any site that addressed

LGBT issues in a positive or informative way was blocked. One of my favorite resources to use with students in their researching of contemporary issues is the "Social Issues" collection of links created by the Multnomah County [Oregon] Library. An examination of the links about same-sex marriage at this public library's site demonstrated that almost all of the sites in the "pro" category were blocked, while almost none of the "con" sites were. . . .

Vain Attempts

I am more fortunate than many who have faced battles with Internet filtering because I had the strong building-level support from Fulton High's executive principal, Dr. Jon Rysewyk. He understands the role of the library in students' success, and appreciates the need for equity and autonomy in students' information seeking. Dr. Rysewyk's consistent support of the Fulton GSA evidences his understanding of the importance of this group in fostering a safe and positive school climate. When I encountered resistance, I could count on Dr. Rysewyk to lend his administrative clout to the contacts I made with those in the upper echelons of instructional leadership in the district. Unfortunately, however, these contacts often led to a frustrating lack of resolution. . . .

Finally, after much active inquiry followed by many passive months of hoping that my earlier inquiries had created a spark somewhere that would ignite change, I was tired of waiting around. On January 21, 2009, I contacted the Nashville-based Tennessee ACLU by mail. I was still hoping to keep the fight to unblock these websites as local as possible. It was not my desire to subject my school or my district to negative publicity, but apparently I needed a voice larger than my own to successfully effect change.

When I heard from ACLU attorney Tricia Herzfeld on January 27, 2009, I assumed that it was in response to my letter; however, during the course of our initial phone conversation, I learned that Herzfeld didn't yet know my letter existed. Students beyond my own at Fulton High School were engaged with this

Internet Use and Health Information

Along with an increasing reliance on the Internet in general, adolescents have increased their use of online resources to answer their health questions. . . . When asked what made the Internet such an important resource, the most frequent response [in a 2002 Kaiser Foundation Survey] was its privacy and confidentiality. This element of confidentiality played a key role in the reason why adolescents felt comfortable using the Internet to access this information, with 82 percent reporting it as the most important reason in using the Internet as a health resource. The results of the study suggest, therefore, that the Internet is increasingly vital for adolescents seeking out health and sexuality information they may be reluctant or unable to access via other means. The importance of privacy may also encourage adolescents to choose to use a library Internet connection rather than one available at home, as they may be under the impression that a public terminal will not keep a record of where they go online. According to the Kaiser report, 58 percent of adolescents reported not being concerned that their online activity would be documented on terminals available at their school or library.

David Brian Holt, *"Internet Filtering and the Gay/Lesbian Patron,"* Library Student Journal, *September 2006.*

issue and working toward a resolution: Andrew Emitt, a senior at Knox County's Central High School, had been searching for information about LGBT scholarships and sent his own letter to the ACLU-TN when he found many of these resources blocked. Andrew knew me from my work with the Fulton GSA; he and some of his classmates had contacted me as a resource for starting a GSA of their own. Andrew named me as a supportive adult in the community who might be willing to lend my input to his challenge of Knox County's filtering policy. Students outside our district in Metropolitan Nashville had contacted ACLU-TN as well. Keila Franks and Emily Logan were both active in their schools' GSAs; I am listed with them and with Fulton High School student and GSA member Bryanna Shelton as plaintiffs in what turned out to be a relatively brief and significantly successful civil case.

The Fight Is On!

The ACLU's research and consultations with student complainants in the Knoxville and Nashville districts, my exploration of websites at school, and the list and descriptions of the blocked categories at the ENA site illustrated that this was not just a case of "keyword" blocking that cast a wide net, scooping up appropriate sites along with inappropriate ones. . . .

On May 19, 2009, the ACLU filed suit in the U.S. District Court for the Middle District of Tennessee against Metropolitan Nashville Public Schools and Knox County Schools. Of the rationale for this civil case, Herzfeld noted, "While schools may have an interest in using filters to block material that could be harmful to minors, blocking access to information about LGBT issues while allowing anti-gay information is unlawful and potentially dangerous. There is no place for this kind of unconstitutional censorship in our public schools."

In response to the suit the LGBT category of websites was unblocked on June 4, 2009. The lawsuit was not officially settled until August 13, 2009, however, because the ACLU wanted assurance in perpetuity of the school districts' agreement to stop using "filtering software that blocks or otherwise places a barrier to student or faculty access to the LGBT sites." If this agreement is broken, the case will return to the court.

The ACLU's response to the results again came from Herzfeld:

> "We're pleased that these schools are finally living up to their legal obligation to allow the free and open exchange of ideas

and information. Schools that censor educational information out of some misguided assumption that anything about LGBT people is automatically sexual or inappropriate are doing a disservice to their students. We are pleased that both school boards in this case have agreed to respect students' rights and refrain from this sort of censorship in the future."

Because of our successful lawsuit, LGBT sites are now unblocked for students in Knox County and Metro Nashville. More significant, however, are the broader implications: Because ENA is the filtering system for 80 percent of the school districts in Tennessee and a comparable number of districts in Indiana, an equitable breadth of information is now available to students in all of them. . . .

Contacting ACLU-TN was the most pragmatic action I could have taken in my role as a school librarian. Access to information is in my job description; there was no question in my mind—I intended to see the process through to the end, whatever that was going to take. The best part of this journey was the spark of student activism it ignited, which is really the reason I do what I do: I place the resources in students' hands so that they can use them to improve their understanding, their lives, and their world. Students like Andrew, Keila, Emily, Bryanna—and all of the supportive adults in their lives—have set a precedent for action and should be commended for their tenacity. As LGBT students embrace these identities at a younger and younger age, they and their peers need access to information that can accurately and sensitively address their questions, as well as create understanding and tolerance in schools rather than judgment and fear.

"I feel so sad for them. They're not thinking about the LGBT kids who need help and can't get it."

A Student Discusses Her Struggle to Gain Access to Online LGBT Information

Personal Narrative

Bryanna Shelton, interviewed by Rose Kennedy

The following viewpoint is an interview with Bryanna Shelton, who, at fifteen years old, participated in a successful lawsuit charging that the school libraries in her Tennessee district were illegally blocking access to websites that offered support for LGBT (lesbian, gay, bisexual and transgender) people. Shelton describes her sudden local fame after the lawsuit, which resulted in hateful comments on local television station websites. She argues that those who condemn her and other gay and lesbian students should think before they speak and offer more support for young people facing difficult questions. Rose Kennedy, the interviewer, is a writer in Knoxville, Tennessee.

When the ACLU [American Civil Liberties Union] filed a lawsuit May 19 [2009] against Knox County Schools [in Tennessee] demanding that it cease and desist filtering educational lesbian, gay, bisexual, and transgender websites on school computers, 15-year-old Bryanna Shelton says she had no fears about being named as one of two Knoxville-based plaintiffs. "First off, I'm out, and second, everybody at my school, Fulton High School, has been nice about it and very supportive," she says. "Plus, I have people to talk to if I need to."

But the television appearances on WBIR and WATE after the news of the suit broke? "Now that was scary!" says Shelton, who prefers goofing off at the lake and chatting on Facebook to answering questions in front of a television camera. "It was nerve-wracking, even though everyone on set was really nice."

Some who commented on the story on the two shows' websites, though, weren't so nice. Remarks on WBIR.com alone number in the 600s, and one particularly galled her: "'Gays, queers, and lesbians should not be allowed to attend the same schools as normal people.' It's just one of the many that are crazy!" she says. "We're not a different species. I'm not gonna rub off on them. They were born what they are, and they're not gonna just wake up like, 'I'm going to start liking girls today.'"

Shelton did post a link to the WATE news segment on her Facebook page, but there a typical comment from about 20 from friends and family read, "You go girl!" and an entire conversation was devoted to whether Shelton did or did not sound country on the video clips ("You saying that I have no accent just kinda made my day!" she writes to a friend). Within a week, a more typical post from her after a trip to the beach reads, "just got back . . . wondering how I can be peeling but have no tan at all?!"

Only three schoolmates seemed to notice she'd even been on the air, says Shelton, and she's convinced that all will be forgotten quickly. "I think by the time next school year comes it won't even be in the news for it to hurt me," she says.

She refuses to let the remarks she has read bother her. "But I think there's at least one gay person in every [extended] family," she says. "So those commenters should really, just . . . watch what they say." And the teen, who is an A student, loves math, and aspires to become a psychologist, notes that she's never had a similar confrontation with an anti-gay adult face to face. "Online, they don't have to live up to what they say. Their face is hidden. They don't think about how I'm just 15, [and] that they're talking about a freshman in high school, telling me I'm so wrong for living this lifestyle. But I didn't choose this; I didn't choose to be born gay."

Lucky to Have Support

The teen was tapped as a plaintiff in the suit because as a ninth grader, she'd still be enrolled in high school if it dragged on, and because she had a support system in place and an accepting school environment.

"I know that one of my teachers isn't for gay people, but that day [after the broadcast] he was like, 'Hey Bryanna, I saw you on television. I'm proud of what you're standing up for!'" Shelton says. "I'm one of the lucky kids I guess. I know at other schools they would have gone through a whole bunch of crap."

Another plus: Shelton had legal permission from her mother, Angie Wright, to participate. "It's very easy for her to be who she is," says Wright, who moved to Knoxville from Pennsylvania about six years ago. ''She has a nice little network of support. She has some friends who can't tell their parents and can't speak up and have to stand by and watch things happen, so she's also speaking for them."

Wright is still plowing through the online comments. "I probably read 30 pages yesterday," she says. "Most are very off-topic. I know this is a very Christian area, but I didn't expect it to be so closed-minded. I thought there would be more of a discussion, but it's really a lot of name-calling."

The commenters who bother her most? "The ones who say, 'Why do these schools even have a GSA [Gay-Straight Alliance]?

SCHOOLS AND GAY-STRAIGHT ALLIANCES

In the 2009 National School Climate Survey of more than 7,000 students, conducted by the Gay Lesbian Straight Education Network, fewer than half of those responding said that their school sponsors a gay-straight alliance (GSA) or similar organization.

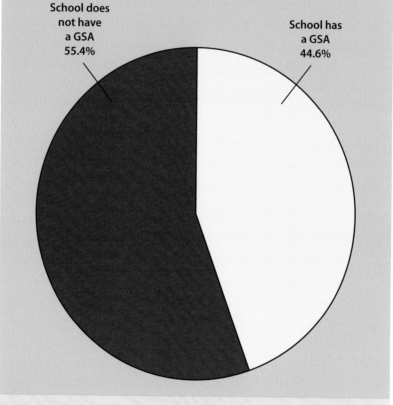

School does not have a GSA 55.4%

School has a GSA 44.6%

Taken from: GLSEN, "Executive Summary," *The 2009 National School Climate Survey,* September 2010.

We should be teaching the Bible in school,'" says Wright. "What they don't seem to realize is that we do have Christian after-school organizations. If that's what their kid chooses, fine. Why shouldn't these other kids be able to have a GSA?"

Wright thinks that some of the negative commenters are able to distance themselves emotionally when they make remarks like, "They want to get to your kids and tell them that a wicked perverted sodomite lifestyle is okay."

"I don't think they remember these are real kids; they're so preoccupied with the concept of gay being right or wrong. I feel so sad for them. They're not thinking about the LGBT kids who need help and can't get it. If a kid wants to go to school and look at Godhatesfags.com, they can, but GLSEN [Gay, Lesbian and Straight Education Network] is blocked. I can just see one of these kids coming home after their parents posted a comment on WBIR, saying, 'Hey, I have something I need some help with.'"

> *"Just because an administrator does not like what a student is posting about faculty or students, he or she does not have authority to impose discipline."*

Teen Internet Use Off-Campus Raises Unsettled Legal Questions

Rosann DiPietro

In the following viewpoint, Rosann DiPietro summarizes several cases in which students were disciplined by school administrators for online material—often offensive material mocking school teachers and other officials—that they created away from school. As DiPietro explains, the courts have worked thoughtfully to determine which of this content is and is not punishable and have generally agreed that schools may not punish students for what they term "off-campus speech" unless the material causes a serious disruption of the school's efforts to teach. Disliking the content or disagreeing with it is not enough, she concludes. DiPietro is an attorney who represents school boards and administrators in all aspects of education law.

Rosann DiPietro, "Constitutional Limitations on a Public School's Authority to Punish Student Internet Speech," *Journal of Internet Law*, vol. 11, no. 12, June 2008, pp. 3, 5–6, 9–10. Reproduced with the permission of Aspen Publishers. Copyright © 2008 Aspen Publishers, Inc. All rights reserved.

With the proliferation of social networking sites, student-created Web sites, instant messaging, and electronic mail, communications that may otherwise have occurred in person, over the telephone, or not at all now exist in retrievable format. Opportunities for school administrators to discover student communications and to be offended thereby have thus increased. In addition, the line between in-school and out-of-school conduct has become blurred with conversations occurring in cyberspace. School officials often have difficulty applying long-standing codes of conduct to new technologies. . . .

It is beyond dispute that Internet communications are "speech" within the First Amendment. . . .

Established case law tells us that students do have free speech rights and that such rights are broader when the expression is not school-sponsored. In *Tinker v. Des Moines Independent Community School District*, Justice [Abe] Fortas famously pointed out that "[i]t can hardly be argued that either students or teachers shed their constitutional rights to freedom of speech or expression at the schoolhouse gate." . . . Under the [1969] *Tinker* decision, schools may impose restrictions on non-school sponsored speech when the speech tends to materially disrupt class work, or involves substantial disorder or invasion of the rights of others, or is reasonably likely to cause disruption or disorder. In *Tinker*, students wore armbands in silent protest to the Vietnam War. The majority was not convinced that any disruption had occurred, although the dissent had a different view of the facts. The Court found that the imposition of discipline violated the students' right of expression, noting that mere dislike of a viewpoint, or an unsubstantiated fear of disruption, would not justify an infringement on free speech rights enjoyed by public school students. . . .

Application to Online Speech Cases

Applying existing case law to the world of online expression is not so easy. In schools, with the use of the school's computer resources, students may view the handiwork of other students. If those expressions, which were created by the student out of school using his or her own computer, nonetheless cause a disruption in school when other students see them, does this give the school officials the sufficient nexus [connection] to impose discipline? It may depend on whether the creator facilitated the exchange of information in the schools. . . .

A [1998] federal court case from the Eastern District of Missouri, *Beussink v. Woodland R-IV School District*, involved a public school student who created his own Web site from home, off school hours and without using any school resources. The homepage was highly critical of the administration of the student's high school. The student used vulgar language to convey his views, and he invited readers to contact the school principal to convey their own opinions. The page also contained a hyperlink that allowed a reader to access the school's homepage from the student's homepage. . . .

Another student, after viewing the student's homepage from his home computer and engaging in an argument over the homepage, deliberately accessed his homepage from the school's computers and showed it to a teacher. It should be noted that the Web site creator did not request that his Web site be viewed from school computers. Also, there was no evidence of any disruption or disorder within the school caused by the existence of this Web site. The principal decided to discipline the student who had created the homepage on the sole basis that the homepage had been displayed in one of the school's classrooms. The student was suspended for five days. For unexplained reasons, the suspension was then lengthened to 10 days.

The court determined that the imposition of discipline violated the student's First Amendment rights. The court noted that, although schools may limit student speech, limitation is permissible only when there is a finding that engaging in the forbidden speech would materially and substantially interfere with the requirements of appropriate discipline in the operation of the school.

In *Emmett v. Kent School District No. 415* [2000], a high school senior posted a Web page on the Internet that was created from his home without using school resources or time. The site was listed as the "unofficial" school Web site and contained a disclaimer that the school did not sponsor the site. The site contained some commentary on school faculty, and it also contained "mock obituaries" of some classmates. The obituaries were tongue-in-cheek and were inspired by a creative writing class assignment the previous year in which students were assigned to write their own obituary. The plaintiff's Web site invited visitors to vote on who would "die" next. A news story featuring the plaintiff's Web site characterized this information as a "hit list." The plaintiff was placed on emergency expulsion for intimidation, harassment, disruption to the educational process, and violation of the school's copyright. The school had no evidence that any student was intimidated by the site or that the plaintiff had intended to intimidate anyone.

The court held that the expulsion violated the student's First Amendment rights. Although students do not have unfettered free speech rights, schools are not entitled to restrict non-school-sponsored speech at will. . . .

Disruption Is the Key

In *J.S. v. Bethlehem Area School District* [2002], the Supreme Court of Pennsylvania upheld the discipline of a student for creating at home and posting on the Internet a Web site that contained derogatory, profane, offensive, and threatening statements directed toward a teacher and a principal. Of note was one of the Web pages listing reasons why the teacher should die and asking for money to help pay for a hit man. The page also contained a cartoon drawing of the teacher with her head cut off and blood dripping from her neck.

The student told other students about the Web site and showed it to another student at school. Believing the threats to be serious, the principal called a faculty meeting and contacted the police and FBI. These law enforcement authorities declined to file charges. However, the principal instituted disciplinary proceedings. Meanwhile, the teacher suffered anxiety from the incident such that she missed the remainder of the school year and obtained a leave of absence the following year. . . .

The court noted that, while the Web site was created off campus, J.S. accessed it at school and showed it to a classmate. The content of the Web site then circulated in the school. The speech was thus considered to be on campus, but not school sponsored. Because the speech caused actual disruption, rather than mild distraction or curiosity, the school district had authority to discipline the student for it. . . .

Doninger v. Niehoff [2008] involved a student who was not suspended but merely disqualified from running for class office because of vulgar and uncivilized comments concerning administrators that were contained in the student's blog. That case is important not so much for its discussion of First Amendment rights, but for the proposition that, when extracurricular activities are concerned, the standard for school administrators is much lower because participation in extracurricular activities is not a constitutionally protected property interest. The School District . . . could disqualify the student in furtherance of legitimate concerns, such as the insistence that its class officers uphold acceptable standards of civility in their communications with faculty. The court stated that the student "does not have a First Amendment right to run for a voluntary extracurricular position as a student leader while engaging in uncivil and offensive communications regarding school administrators." In contrast, if a student were disciplined for uncivil discourse with an administrator that caused no disruption or disorder, such discipline would likely be unsuccessful in the face of a First Amendment challenge. Merely offensive speech . . . cannot be proscribed.

The final case discussed in this section, *Wisniewski v. Board of Education of Weedsport Central School District* [2007], involved instant messaging, which permits students to communicate real-

As more and more students bring mobile devices into the classroom, schools are increasingly dealing with offensive text messages and online postings. © Thomas Barwick/Taxi/Getty Images.

time with others online. The particular product used by this student, AOL, permits the transmission of an icon along with the text of an instant message, so that every message sent by the user is accompanied by this icon. In this particular case, the chosen icon depicted a pistol firing a bullet at a person's head with dots above it representing splattered blood. The icon was accompanied by the words "Kill Mr. VanderMolen," who was the student's teacher. The icon was not sent to the teacher or any other school official. The student kept this icon for approximately three weeks. During this time, it came to the attention of a classmate, who informed the teacher. The student was suspended for five days. The police determined that the icon was merely a joke, as did a psychologist who evaluated the student.

The court upheld the grant of summary judgment in favor of the School District, finding that the icon with the caption could reasonably be construed as a threat and thus was not entitled to First Amendment protections. . . . The court found it reasonably likely that the icon would come to the attention of school authorities and that it would materially and substantially disrupt the work and discipline of the school. The icon was distributed to 15 recipients, including some classmates, during its three-week transmission period, making it foreseeable, if not inevitable, that the icon would make its way to the target. Once made known to the teacher, the court found it reasonably foreseeable that disruption within the school environment would occur. That the icon did not constitute a criminal threat and was not created at school were not dispositive [determining] factors for the court.

School Districts Must Not Overreact

This collection of First Amendment cases provides useful guidance to administrators who, if they have not already, will likely soon face a situation in which a student has electronically communicated something unpleasant or downright alarming about a member of the school community. The decisions suggest that, unless students are doing something like orchestrating a mass viewing of their Web sites from school computers or advocating violence against a student, teacher, or school property, school districts can do little to stop students from posting information or sending electronic mail or instant messages on their own time

"Please excuse Harold for not having his homework. His Internet service provider's servers were down and he couldn't connect to his online homework helpline."

"Please excuse Harold for not having his homework. His Internet service provider's servers were down and he couldn't conntect to his onlne homework helpline," Aaron Bacall. CartoonStock.com

using their own computers. The courts have consistently stressed that, just because an administrator does not like what a student is posting about faculty or students, he or she does not have authority to impose discipline. In addition, the fact that technology now allows easy access to Web pages from other locations does not alone give schools the authority to impose discipline. If specific threats or the equivalent of an assault is made, disruption or disorder in the school occurs, or the online speech is uttered "at school," administrators would have authority to act. The cases are not entirely consistent with one another, but the courts appear willing to grant more slack in cases involving violent themes.

It bears repeating that online expression having no demonstrated effect on school order cannot form the basis of discipline unless a student has used school resources to express himself or herself. In that case, a school district may wish to make a case based on misuse of school resources rather than the content of the expression. For example, if a student is using school resources to edit, exhibit, or view his or her own online creations or to transmit electronic mail messages that have no relation to the educational mission, school officials may punish such conduct if it violates provisions of a student handbook or Internet acceptable use policy. By now, such policies routinely prohibit electronic mail communications or access to Web sites that have no educational value or purpose. Some list specific Web sites that many students are not permitted to view, including MySpace, Facebook, and other social networking sites. Again, schools must be careful not to squelch expressions of controversial viewpoints, simply because those views are controversial.

> "The inability of public schools to
> discipline a student for improper
> conduct . . . would seriously hamper
> a school's efforts to advance the
> educational mission."

Schools Should Be Able to Discipline Students for Off-Campus Internet Use

Sean A. Fields

In the following viewpoint, attorney Sean A. Fields, representing the Pennsylvania School Boards Association (PSBA), argues that schools must be allowed to discipline students for certain offensive content created online, even if that content was created away from school. The viewpoint was presented to the Court of Appeals as an amicus curiae, or "friend-of-the-court," brief, as the PSBA wished to express its support for one of its member districts. The district had been told by the District Court that it should not have disciplined a student, Justin Layshock, for creating a parody MySpace page that made fun of his school principal. The decision in Layshock v. Hermitage School District *(2007) was wrong, Fields argues, because it took away the authority a school must have to protect its students and staff and to fulfill its responsibility to teach students where the boundaries between acceptable and unacceptable behavior lie.*

Sean A. Fields, Brief of Amicus Curiae, *Layshock v. Hermitage School District*, US Court of Appeals for the Third District, April 4, 2008, Docket No. 07-4465. To help students more easily access the brief, subheads have been inserted and minor edits have been made to the brief.

PSBA [the Pennsylvania School Boards Association] files this brief for the purpose of providing this Honorable Court with the perspective of public school districts in Pennsylvania. This case involves the unique issue of a school district's authority to discipline a student for the creation of a mock MySpace profile that misused a school administrator's likeness; used lewd and offensive language; and was targeted to the school community in a manner that undermined the educational mission of the school district. Due to the proliferation of technology in the current school environment, it is important that public schools maintain their traditionally recognized authority.

The inability of public schools to discipline a student for improper conduct involving speech or expression simply because the expression was created off-campus would seriously hamper a school's efforts to advance the educational mission of teaching children about exercising personal responsibility in preparation for participation in our democratic civil society. The authority of school districts to discipline members of the school community for expressions intruding upon the rights of others is crucial to preserving the safety of students and school employees. Moreover, the discipline of a student who improperly uses the likeness of an administrator to create a profile that is lewd, offensive, profane, or defamatory is not shielded by the First Amendment. Therefore, PSBA respectfully asks this Honorable Court to articulate a test [that is, to state a rule] that maintains the school district's authority and reverses the decision of the lower court. . . .

Not All Speech Is Protected

It is a well-established principal of constitutional jurisprudence that certain forms of speech are not subject to the protections of the First Amendment. In the school context, speech that is lewd, obscene or profane is not protected speech. . . . The Court [has] recognized the importance of prohibiting the use of vulgar and offensive terms in public discourse concluding the First Amendment does not prevent school officials from determining

Can a Blog Post Lead to Discipline?

We begin with some basic principles of First Amendment law. While students do not "shed their constitutional rights to freedom of speech or expression at the schoolhouse gate," *Tinker v. Des Moines Indep. Cmty. Sch. Dist.* (1969), the constitutional rights of students in public school "are not automatically coextensive with the rights of adults in other settings," *Bethel Sch. Dist. No. 403 v. Fraser* (1986). Instead, these rights must be applied in a manner consistent with the "special characteristics of the school environment," *Tinker.* Thus, school administrators may prohibit student expression that will "materially and substantially disrupt the work and discipline of the school," *Tinker.* Because schools have a responsibility for "teaching students the boundaries of socially appropriate behavior," *Fraser*, offensive speech that would receive full constitutional protection if used by an adult in public discourse may, consistent with the First Amendment, give rise to disciplinary action by a school, *Fraser.* Additionally, educators are permitted to exercise editorial control over "school-sponsored expressive activities such as school publications or theatrical productions," *Doninger II*, so long as their actions are "reasonably related to legitimate pedagogical concerns," *Hazelwood Sch. Dist. v. Kuhlmeier* (1988). Finally, and most recently, the Supreme Court has determined that public schools may "take steps to safeguard those entrusted to their care from speech that can reasonably be regarded as encouraging illegal drug use," *Morse v. Frederick* (2007), because of the special nature of the school environment and the dangers posed by student drug uses.

> *Debra Ann Livingston, Circuit judge opinion,*
> Doninger v. Niehoff, *United States Court of*
> *Appeals for the Second Circuit, April 25, 2011,*
> *p. 14.*

that to permit obscene, profane or plainly offensive speech would undermine the school's basic educational mission. The kind of speech [student Justin] Layshock used in creating the MySpace profile [mocking his principal], is the class of speech that public schools have traditionally disciplined students for without breaching the boundaries of protected speech under the First Amendment.

Layshock's characterizations of Principal [Eric] Trosch strike a tone that is patently . . . offensive. . . . Layshock's use of terms such as, "big hard-on," "big dick," and "big whore" amount to speech that is "wholly inconsistent with the 'fundamental values' of public education." Although . . . Layshock's audience was not a captive audience, the school community was the target audience of the profile. Because of the nexus [connection] between the profile and the school community, Justin's speech was subject to the disciplinary policies of the District.

There is a wide chasm between the political expression of students who passively demonstrate opposition to a war or thoughtfully criticize a school's disciplinary policy and Layshock's profile. Layshock's profile does not provide any commentary or political statement on the management of the school district or the conduct of Eric Trosch as a school administrator. It is simply a crass attempt to ridicule a school official through the use of language devoid of any social or political value. Restrictions on the content of speech are permissible in areas which are "of such slight social value as a step to truth that any benefit that may be derived from them is clearly outweighed by the social interest in order and morality," *Chaplinsky v. New Hampshire* (1942).

Students May Not Disrupt the Educational Process

Even assuming *arguendo* [for the sake of argument] that Layshock's speech was not obscene, profane or plainly offensive, the impact of the profile did create a substantial and material disruption to the educational process sufficient to satisfy the requirements of *Tinker* [*v. Des Moines Independent Community School District* (1969), the case that defined students' First Amendment rights] and its progeny. *Tinker* does not stand for the proposition that students have free reign to openly insult teachers and administrators using offensive language by smearing an administrator by using mean-spirited epithets.

Layshock's profile promotes illegal drug and alcohol abuse at the expense of an authority figure contrary to the school's educational mission of promoting personal responsibility. Applying the rights of a student "in light of the special characteristics of the school environment," means balancing the student's interest in the right to free speech against the school's interest in promoting the well-being of the students by maintaining an atmosphere of discipline and respect of self and others. In *Morse v. Frederick* [2007], the U.S. Supreme Court held that schools have the authority to regulate speech that can reasonably be regarded as encouraging illegal drug use. The message in the *Morse* case was simply, "BONG HITS 4 JESUS." Layshock's profile depicts Trosch as a user of "steroids," "pills," and "blunts." Therefore, the speech suggests that a school authority figure uses illegal drugs in the form of steroids and marijuana. Even if other students in the school community were aware the profile was created by another student who did not intend to promote drug use, the message is one that is within the school district's authority to regulate.

In addition to the pedagogical concerns of teaching students about civility and taking responsibility for respecting boundaries, public schools must be mindful of protecting the rights of the members of the school community who may fall prey to statements that are defamatory or constitute unlawful harassment. Layshock's speech is not protected under the First Amendment because it invades the rights of others. The *Tinker* court reasoned that conduct or speech by a student involving "substantial disorder or *invasion of the rights of others*" is not immunized by the First Amendment.

Mocking school officials online has much more far-reaching consequences than traditional ways of self-expression. © Doris Day/Archive Photos/Getty Images.

Defamation Is Not Protected

In addition to First Amendment jurisprudence, the Pennsylvania State Board of Education regulations acknowledge recognized legal boundaries of student speech. "Students have a responsibility to obey laws governing libel and obscenity and to be aware of the full meaning of their expression." Therefore, Pennsylvania's regulations prohibit a student from expressing speech that is defamatory. A communication is defamatory if it "tends so to harm the reputation of another as to lower him in the estimation of the community or to deter third persons from association or dealing with him." The Supreme Court has stated that to be libelous, a statement does not necessarily have to be universally regarded as such, or even regarded as such by a majority of people in the community. It is enough to be considered libel if the statement hurts the party alluded to "in the estimation of an important and respectable part of the community," *Peck v. Tribune Co.*, (1909). . . .

Defamation injures the reputation and diminishes the esteem, respect, goodwill or confidence the plaintiff held, or excites adverse, derogatory or unpleasant feelings or opinions against him.

The impact of Layshock's profile goes well beyond the juvenile ridicule that students traditionally communicated among the student community in paper notes passed among students. The answers in the profile have a real capacity to undermine Trosch's authority and standing in the Hermitage School District community, as well as an endless list of potential viewers in cyberspace that may include other education professionals and prospective employers.

Layshock's comments and the forum he used to express those comments have the capacity to damage Trosch's reputation as well as create a school atmosphere where students may insult, offend, defame or harass administrators, teachers, and students with impunity. The Supreme Court has "repeatedly emphasized the need for affirming the comprehensive authority of the States and of school officials, consistent with fundamental constitutional safeguards, to prescribe and control conduct in the schools," *Tinker*. "Without first establishing discipline and maintaining order, teachers cannot begin to educate their students," *New Jersey v. T.L.O.* (1985).

Schools Must Teach Boundaries

It would be myopic to view Layshock's profile as a silly joke confined to the relatively small confines of Hermitage School District. Although the profile was directed at the school community,

Layshock became a publisher of content without geographical boundaries when the profile was posted on MySpace. The tone and impact of Layshock's comments must be considered within the context of the educational mission of the school. Part of that educational mission includes protecting the rights of students as well as school employees. Fortunately, Layshock did not subject a fellow student to the ugly characterizations aimed at Trosch. This is the context for public schools exercising responsible discipline to teach children boundaries as well as to protect others.

Current news headlines illustrate the challenges facing the school community. At Parkland High School [in Allentown, Pennsylvania] at least two students took nude pictures of themselves which were passed by students around the school on camera. In Philadelphia, a camera phone captured an attack of a disabled child while a group of students watched laughing. The video was then posted to the assaulted student's MySpace page against his will. In another tragic case, a thirteen year-old student hanged herself in her bedroom closet after a cruel cyber hoax involving another student and the student's mother. The kind of conduct Justin engaged in did not target other students. However, the examples illustrate the importance of the ability of public schools to discipline in instances where students go beyond the boundaries of protected speech by intruding upon the rights of others.

From a public policy perspective it would be untenable for this Honorable Court to articulate a rule permitting a student to direct speech at the school community in a manner that invades the rights of others. Such a rule would undermine the ability of public school districts to provide an environment where both students and teachers feel secure enough to advance the goals of the school community.

> *"It would be an unseemly and dangerous precedent to allow the state, in the guise of school authorities, to reach into a child's home and control his/her actions."*

Schools May Not Punish Students for Most Off-Campus Internet Speech

The District Appeals Court's Decision

Theodore A. McKee

In February 2010, separate three-judge panels of the US Court of Appeals, Third District, made rulings in two cases involving Pennsylvania students who created fake MySpace pages making fun of their school principals. In Layshock v. Hermitage School District, *the Court ruled that the school had no legal right to punish the student for his admittedly offensive parody; in* J.S. v. Blue Mountain School District, *the Court ruled that the student's rights were not violated when the school disciplined her. To settle the confusion resulting from the two decisions, the Court agreed to hear both cases again,* en banc *(or with the full roster of judges). On June 13, 2011, the Court issued rulings declaring that in both cases the students' punishment violated the First Amendment. In the following viewpoint, Chief Judge Theodore McKee writes that schools*

Theodore A. McKee, Opinion of the Court, *Layshock v. Hermitage School District*, US Court of Appeals for the Third District, June 13, 2011.

generally may not discipline students for their out-of-school speech unless it creates a "substantial" disruption. The Courts will handle illegal speech, he argues, but punishing legal speech created by minors is up to parents.

W e are asked to determine if a school district can punish a student for expressive conduct that originated outside of the schoolhouse, did not disturb the school environment and was not related to any school sponsored event. We hold that, under these circumstances, the First Amendment prohibits the school from reaching beyond the schoolyard to impose what might otherwise be appropriate discipline. . . .

Creating a Fake Profile

In December of 2005, Justin Layshock was a seventeen-year-old senior at Hickory High School, which is part of the Hermitage School District in Hermitage, Pennsylvania. Sometime between December 10th and 14th, 2005, while Justin was at his grandmother's house during non-school hours, he used her computer to create what he would later refer to as a "parody profile" of his Principal, Eric Trosch. The only school resource that was even arguably involved in creating the profile was a photograph of Trosch that Justin copied from the School District's website. Justin copied that picture with a simple "cut and paste" operation using the computer's internet browser and mouse. Justin created the profile on "MySpace." . . .

Justin created the profile by giving bogus answers to survey questions taken from various templates that were designed to assist in creating a profile. The survey included questions about favorite shoes, weaknesses, fears, one's idea of a "perfect pizza," bedtime, etc. All of Justin's answers were based on a theme of "big," because Trosch is apparently a large man. . . .

Justin afforded access to the profile to other students in the School District by listing them as "friends" on the MySpace website, thus allowing them to view the profile. Not surprisingly, word of the profile "spread like wildfire" and soon reached most, if not all, of Hickory High's student body.

During mid-December 2005, three other students also posted unflattering profiles of Trosch on MySpace. Each of those profiles was more vulgar and more offensive than Justin's. Trosch first learned about one of the other profiles from his daughter, who was in eleventh grade. . . .

The Adults' Reactions

Trosch believed all of the profiles were "degrading," "demeaning," "demoralizing," and "shocking." He was also concerned about his reputation and complained to the local police. Although he was not concerned for his safety, he was interested in pressing charges against those responsible for the bogus profiles, and he discussed whether the first profile he discovered might constitute harassment, defamation, or slander. However, no criminal charges were ever filed against Justin or any of the other student authors of profiles.

On December 15th, Justin used a computer in his Spanish classroom to access his MySpace profile of Trosch. He also showed it to other classmates, although he did not acknowledge his authorship. After viewing the profile, the students logged off of MySpace. Justin again attempted to access the profile from school on December 16th, purportedly to delete it. School district administrators were unaware of Justin's in-school attempts to access MySpace until their investigation the following week. Teacher Craig Antush glimpsed the profile in his computer lab class and told the students who were congregating around a computer and giggling to shut it down. . . .

Justin's parents were understandably upset over Justin's behavior. They discussed the matter with him, expressed their extreme disappointment, "grounded" him, and prohibited him from using their home computer.

On January 3, 2006, the school district sent a letter to Justin and his parents giving them notice of an informal hearing that was to be held. The letter read, in pertinent part, as follows:

> Justin admitted prior to the informal hearing that he created a profile about Mr. Trosch. This infraction is a violation of the Hermitage School District Discipline Code: Disruption of the normal school process; Disrespect; Harassment of a school administrator via computer/internet with remarks that have demeaning implications; Gross misbehavior; Obscene, vulgar and profane language; Computer Policy violations (use of school pictures without authorization).

The School District subsequently found Justin guilty of all of those charges.

In addition to a ten-day, out-of-school suspension, Justin's punishment consisted of (1) being placed in the Alternative Education Program (the "ACE" program) at the high school for the remainder of the 2005–2006 school year; (2) being banned from all extracurricular activities, including Academic Games and foreign-language tutoring; and (3) not being allowed to participate in his graduation ceremony. The Layshocks were also informed that the School District was considering expelling Justin. Ironically, Justin, who created the least vulgar and offensive profile, and who was the only student to apologize for his behavior, was also the only student punished for the MySpace profiles.

The Layshocks initiated this action on January 27, 2006, by filing a three count complaint. . . . Count I of the complaint alleged that the District's punishment of Justin violated his rights under the First Amendment. . . .

The First Amendment's Application in Public Schools

In the landmark case of *Tinker v. Des Moines Indep. Cmty. Sch. Dist.* (1969), a group of high school students decided to wear

J.S. v. Blue Mountain
School District

J.S., a minor, by and through her parents, Terry Snyder and Steven Snyder, individually and on behalf of their daughter, appeal the District Court's grant of summary judgment in favor of the Blue Mountain School District ("the School District") and denial of their motion for summary judgment. This case arose when the School District suspended J.S. for creating, on a weekend and on her home computer, a MySpace profile (the "profile") making fun of her middle school principal, James McGonigle. The profile contained adult language and sexually explicit content. J.S. and her parents sued the School District . . . alleging that the suspension violated J.S.'s First Amendment free speech rights. . . . Because J.S. was suspended from school for speech that indisputably caused no substantial disruption in school and that could not reasonably have led school officials to forecast substantial disruption in school, the School District's actions violated J.S.'s First Amendment free speech rights. We will accordingly reverse and remand that aspect of the District Court's judgment.

Michael Chagares, Chief Judge, J.S. v. Blue Mountain School District, *United States Court of Appeals for the Third Circuit, June 13, 2011.*

black arm bands to school to protest the war in Vietnam. When school officials learned of the planned protest, they preemptively prohibited students from wearing armbands. Several students who ignored the ban and wore armbands to school anyway were suspended. Those students brought an action against the school through their parents, alleging that their First Amendment rights had been violated. The district court rejected that claim and upheld the constitutionality of the school officials' action, finding that it had been reasonable to preserve discipline. The district court's decision was affirmed without opinion by an equally divided court of appeals sitting *en banc* [with the full panel of judges].

The case was appealed to the [US] Supreme Court, which held that student expression may not be suppressed unless school officials reasonably conclude that it will "materially and substantially disrupt the work and discipline of the school." The Court concluded that the students were doing nothing more than engaging in political speech, and wearing armbands to express "their disapproval of the Vietnam hostilities and their advocacy of a truce, to make their views known, and, by their example, to influence others to adopt them." The school district's only interest in banning the speech had been the "mere desire to avoid the discomfort and unpleasantness that always accompany an unpopular viewpoint" or "an urgent wish to avoid the controversy which might result from the expression." The Court held that this interest was not enough to justify banning "a silent, passive expression of opinion, unaccompanied by any disorder or disturbance." In one of its most famous passages, the Court explained:

> First Amendment rights, applied in light of the special characteristics of the school environment, are available to teachers and students. It can hardly be argued that either students or teachers shed their constitutional rights to freedom of speech or expression at the schoolhouse gate. . . .

We realize, of course, that it is now well established that *Tinker's* "schoolhouse gate" is not constructed solely of the bricks and mortar surrounding the school yard. Nevertheless, the concept of the "school yard" is not without boundaries and the reach of school authorities is not without limits. . . .

It would be an unseemly and dangerous precedent to allow the state, in the guise of school authorities, to reach into a child's home and control his/her actions there to the same extent that it can control that child when he/she participates in school spon-

The US Court of Appeals ruled in 2011 that a student's parody website of his school principal is covered by free speech because it was created off-campus. © Rana Faure/Riser/Getty Images.

sored activities. Allowing the District to punish Justin for conduct he engaged in while at his grandmother's house using his grandmother's computer would create just such a precedent, and we therefore conclude that the district court correctly ruled that the District's response to Justin's expressive conduct violated the First Amendment guarantee of free expression. . . .

Was the Fake Profile Disruptive?

The School District also claims that Justin's speech can be treated as "on-campus" speech because it "was aimed at the School District community and the Principal and was accessed on campus by Justin [and] [i]t was reasonably foreseeable that the profile would come to the attention of the School District and the Principal." . . .

In the School District's view, Justin's speech—his MySpace profile of Trosch—was unquestionably vulgar, lewd and offensive, and therefore not shielded by the First Amendment because it ended up inside the school community. . . . Similarly, the School District argues that . . . there is no First Amendment protection for lewd, vulgar, indecent or plainly offensive speech in school. . . .

As noted earlier, the District's January 3, 2006, letter to the Layshocks advising them of Justin's suspension reads, in relevant part, that it was punishing Justin because "Justin admitted prior to the informal hearing that he created a profile about Mr. Trosch." Although the letter also mentions disruption, we have taken care to stress that the District does not now challenge the district court's finding that Justin's conduct did not result in any substantial disruption. Moreover, when pressed at oral argument, counsel for the School District conceded that the District was relying solely on the fact that Justin created the profile of Trosch, and not arguing that it created any substantial disruption in the school. . . . Moreover, we have found no authority that would support punishment for creating such a profile unless it results in foreseeable and substantial disruption of school. . . .

We need not now define the precise parameters of when the arm of authority can reach beyond the schoolhouse gate because, as we noted earlier, the district court found that Justin's conduct did not disrupt the school, and the District does not appeal that finding. Thus, we need only hold that Justin's use of the District's web site does not constitute entering the school, and that the District is not empowered to punish his out of school expressive conduct under the circumstances here.

Based on those two conclusions, we will affirm the district court's grant of summary judgment to Justin Layshock on his First Amendment claim.

> *"For those who support the First Amendment rights of student journalists, this is a positive and important development."*

The District Appeals Court's Rulings on Off-Campus Speech Clarify and Protect Student Rights

Frank LoMonte

LoMonte analyzes two decisions regarding students' off-campus speech that were handed down by the Third US Circuit Court of Appeals on June 13, 2011. The Court revisited two earlier cases— Layshock v. Hermitage School District *and* J.S. v. Blue Mountain School District*—and ruled that in both cases schools were wrong to punish students for creating parody MySpace pages that made fun of their school principals. The new decisions are welcome, LoMonte contends, because they clarify several conditions under which students cannot be disciplined by their schools for online content they create away from school. But, he argues, the Court has failed to resolve the central issue of whether schools are ever permitted to regulate off-campus speech. Resolution, he predicts, will come in the future when the US Supreme Court hears one or both cases.*

LoMonte, formerly an award-winning investigative journalist, is executive director of the Student Press Law Center.

Young people's near-universal ability to publish online—anytime, anywhere—has provoked a flurry of legislative responses and judicial pronouncements, many of them blurring the boundaries that once confined schools' disciplinary authority within the proverbial "schoolhouse gate."

Those blurry boundaries are in somewhat clearer focus today [June 16, 2011] as a result of a pair of rulings by the 3rd U.S. Circuit Court of Appeals, which sent an unmistakable message that schools may not lightly extend their reach into students' off-hours activities.

In two companion rulings issued Monday, the Philadelphia-based court decided that school officials overreached when they suspended two Pennsylvania students, one in high school and one in middle school, for creating mock MySpace profiles ridiculing their principals. The cases, *Layshock v. Hermitage School District* and *J.S. v. Blue Mountain School District*, represent the first time that the issue of school authority over off-campus online speech has come before an *en banc* appeals court comprised of all of the circuit's active judges.

The relatively rare *en-banc* hearing was necessitated when separate three-judge panels of the circuit—in rulings issued on the same day in February 2010—reached differing outcomes on the seemingly indistinguishable cases: the *Layshock* panel found the student's First Amendment rights violated, and the *J.S.* panel saw no violation.

Monday's rulings harmonized these discordant rulings by handing both students a victory that, unless the U.S. Supreme Court elects to hear either or both cases, will stand as final.

Where Is the Line?

For those who support the First Amendment rights of student journalists, this is a positive and important development, even if

YOUTH AND SOCIAL NETWORK SITES

According to a 2009 survey by the Pew Research Center, 73 percent of American youth aged 12 to 17 who went online used social network websites. In 2006, only 55 percent were visiting social network sites.

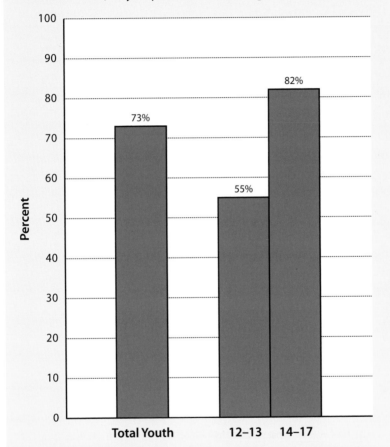

Taken from: Amanda Lenhart, Kristen Purcell, Aaron Smith, and Kathryn Zickhur. "Social Media and Young Adults," Pew Internet and American Life Project, February 3, 2010.

the speech in these cases—childish ridicule about the principal's weight, penis size and sexual proclivities—is hardly "journalistic." A contrary ruling would have emboldened schools to assert control over any criticism of the school or its officials made in any medium, even a letter-to-the-editor of the local newspaper or a speech in front of the Board of Education. If even speech of this dubious value falls within the First Amendment, then students can rest comfortably that editorial commentary will be protected as well.

What the Third Circuit did not do—and what no circuit has yet managed to satisfactorily do—is to create a legal standard to guide all future exercises of discipline over off-campus online speech.

Two competing views are emerging as to when it is proper for schools to punish speech that occurs outside of school premises and school functions.

One school of thought says that, when students leave the campus and are not taking part in a school activity, their speech is governed by the same legal standards as any other citizen's speech. They cannot threaten people with violence, commit libel or steal copyright-protected property without consequences, but otherwise, their speech is beyond the reach of government regulation, including that of schools.

Five of the circuit's 14 judges signed onto a concurring opinion in the *J.S.* case, authored by Judge D. Brooks Smith, that fully embraced this protective legal standard, which is the one supported by the students' lawyers and by the SPLC [Student Press Law Center].

Six of the 14 judges signed onto a dissenting opinion in the *J.S.* case that urged the adoption of a less protective standard—the same standard that applies to speech uttered on school grounds during the school day. That standard, set forth in the Supreme Court's landmark *Tinker v. Des Moines Independent Community School District* [(1969)] ruling, enables schools to prevent or punish student speech if it threatens a substantial disruption of school functions, even if the speech would otherwise fall within the First Amendment.

(In fact, the concurring judges suggested that the majority ruling in fact did recognize *Tinker* as the applicable standard, though the majority claimed to be doing no such thing.)

Some argue that clearer legal standards need to be established for future cases involving students' off-campus Internet postings that involve school officials or other students. © Brendan O'Sullivan/Photolibrary/Getty Images.

Off-Campus Speech and
Tinker Unresolved

To First Amendment experts, the *Tinker* standard is pretty clearly unsuited to off-campus speech for this reason: *Tinker* is about speech to a captive audience of school listeners who cannot leave. We accept that students' First Amendment rights on school premises within the school day are more limited than they are in the "real world," because a student who wears a swastika T-shirt to school is forcing his classmates to see that symbol all day long. But if the swastika is on a student's off-campus web page, viewers must affirmatively seek it out and can easily avert their eyes.

The Smith concurrence eloquently explains the perils of giving school administrators the *Tinker* level of control over what students say outside of the school day:

> Suppose a high school student, while at home after school hours, were to write a blog entry defending gay marriage. Suppose further that several of the student's classmates got wind of the entry, took issue with it, and caused a significant disturbance at school. While the school could clearly punish the students who acted disruptively, if *Tinker* were held to apply to off-campus speech, the school could also punish the student whose blog entry brought about the disruption. That cannot be, nor is it, the law.

The majority in the *J.S.* case did not find it necessary to decide whether the *Tinker* rule or the "real world" rule is the right one for students' online speech, because even under the more school-friendly *Tinker* standard, the student's My Space page was so over-the-top ridiculous that no reasonable person could have taken it seriously (and indeed, no disruptive activity occurred).

While the circuit failed to conclusively resolve the central jurisdictional issue, some important secondary issues were resolved in favor of students' rights.

The Court Clarifies the Boundaries

First, the Circuit seems solidly united behind the proposition that schools may not punish off-campus speech merely because it uses crude and offensive imagery. In *Bethel School District v. Fraser* [(1986)], the Supreme Court empowered schools to punish students for using "lewd" language at school events even if no disruption is foreseeable. That, not *Tinker*, was the school district's basis for claiming jurisdiction over Justin Layshock's MySpace creation. But not a single Third Circuit judge was willing to extend *Fraser* to off-campus activity.

Second, the fact that speech is brought onto campus by third parties is not enough to transform it into "on-campus speech" for purposes of school jurisdiction. In neither the *Layshock* nor the *J.S.* case was there any evidence that the student creators themselves used school time to show off their MySpace handiwork to their classmates. (Indeed, in the *J.S.* case, the only way that the mock profile physically entered the campus is that the student's principal demanded a copy of it.) This is an exceptionally significant distinction, because it is always foreseeable that a member of the audience might transport a copy of off-campus speech onto the campus. At least in the majority's view, that foreseeability by itself does not mean online speech is functionally equivalent to in-school speech.

Third, the fact that the school itself overreacts to a student's speech cannot be bootstrapped into a "disruption" for purposes of satisfying the *Tinker* standard; the disruption must arise out of how listeners react to the speech, not how the school decides to punish it. (In the *J.S.* case, the school actually tried to argue that the student's lawsuit was itself a party of the disruption, leaving aside the inconvenient fact that the punishment predated the lawsuit by several months and that the lawsuit became necessary only because of the punishment.)

And finally, context matters. When adults talk about students' online speech, they invariably talk about how electronically transmitted speech is categorically "worse" and "more dangerous" than speech on the printed page. A lot of this is over-blown—try finding a letter-to-the-editor from an online news-paper that's more than a year old, and you're quite likely to get a "file not found" broken link, but the same letter is retrievable from the archives in the public library for centuries to come. But the Third Circuit recognized, correctly, that reasonable readers do not visit MySpace.com as a source of scholarly research. There is a difference between content that is widely accessible and con-tent that is widely trusted and believed.

School attorneys undoubtedly will attempt to appeal only the *J.S.* case and not the *Layshock* case to the Supreme Court, since the *J.S.* case more squarely raised the *Tinker* issue and since the *J.S.* facts (the speaker was a middle-schooler, while Justin Layshock was a high school senior) are more sympathetic to the school. The close 8-6 split among circuit judges may tempt the Court to accept the case. But the Court typically does not wade into the early stages of an evolving area of the law until the lower courts have thoroughly aired it, and this issue may be sufficiently unsettled to counsel in favor of caution.

> "Today, virtually no one, particularly
> technology savvy students, can claim
> not to know that the online 'sharing'
> of copyrighted music, movies, software
> and other works is illegal."

Those Who Illegally Download Music Should Be Prosecuted

Mitch Bainwol and Cary Sherman

In the viewpoint that follows, music industry executives Mitch Bainwol and Cary Sherman explain why the Recording Industry Association of America (RIAA) began a series of well-publicized lawsuits against college students in 2007, suing them for illegally downloading music. College students are more likely than others to download music and movies illegally, they contend, and colleges and universities are in a good position to teach students ethical and legal behavior and to use technology to block illegal downloading over their campus networks. The industry has tried to educate students and college information technology departments about how to prevent illegal activity but with little success. The authors conclude that college administrators must accept responsibility for managing the problems of illegal downloading on their campuses. Bainwol is chairman and CEO and Sherman is president of the RIAA.

Mitch Bainwol and Cary Sherman, "Explaining the Crackdown on Student Downloading," *Inside Higher Ed*, March 15, 2007. Copyright © 2007 Recording Industry Association of America (RIAA). All rights reserved.

Explaining the Crackdown on Student Downloading
March 15, 2007

As many in the higher education community are well aware from news coverage here and elsewhere, the Recording Industry Association of America (RIAA), on behalf of its member labels, recently initiated a new process for lawsuits against computer users who engage in illegal file-trafficking of copyrighted content on peer-to-peer (P2P) systems. In the new round of lawsuits, 400 of these legal actions were directed at college and university students around the country. The inclusion of so many students was unprecedented. Unfortunately, it was also necessary.

In the three and a half years since we first began suing individuals for illegal file-trafficking, we have witnessed an immense growth in national awareness of this problem. Today [2007] virtually no one, particularly technology savvy students, can claim not to know that the online "sharing" of copyrighted music, movies, software and other works is illegal. By now, there is broad understanding of the impact from this activity, including billions of dollars in lost revenue, millions of dollars in lost taxes, thousands of lost jobs, and entire industries struggling to grow viable legitimate online market places that benefit consumers against a backdrop of massive theft.

We have made great progress—both in holding responsible the illicit businesses profiting from copyright infringement and in deterring many individuals from engaging in illegal downloading behavior. Nevertheless, illegal file-trafficking remains a significant and disproportionate problem on college campuses. A recent survey by *Student Monitor,* from spring 2006, found that more than half of college students download music and movies illegally, and according to the market research firm NPD, college students alone accounted for more than 1.3 billion illegal music downloads in 2006.

Mitch Bainwol, chief executive of the Recording Industry Association of America, outside the US Supreme Court during hearings for a case involving copyright infringement in 2005. © AP Images/Gerald Herbert.

A Teachable Moment

We know some in the university community believe these figures overstate the contribution of college students to the illegal file-trafficking problem today. Yet new data confirms that students are more prone to engaging in this illegal activity than the population at large. While college students represented only 10 percent of the sample in the online NPD study, they accounted for 26 percent of all music downloading on P2P networks and 21 percent of all P2P users in 2006. Furthermore, college students surveyed by NPD reported that more than two-thirds of all the music they acquired was obtained illegally.

Moreover, our focus on university students is not detracting from our continuing enforcement efforts against individuals using commercial Internet Service Provider (ISP) accounts to engage in this same behavior. Indeed, we have asked ISPs to participate in the same new process that we have implemented for university network users.

Yet this is about far more than the size of a particular slice of the pie. This is about a generation of music fans. College students used to be the music industry's best customers. Now, finding a record store still in business anywhere near a campus is a difficult assignment at best. It's not just the loss of current sales that concerns us, but the habits formed in college that will stay with these students for a lifetime. This is a teachable moment—an opportunity to educate these particular students about the importance of music in their lives and the importance of respecting and valuing music as intellectual property.

The prevalence of this activity on our college campuses should be as unacceptable to universities as it is to us. These networks are intended for educational and research purposes. These are the environments where students receive the guidance necessary to become responsible citizens. Institutions of higher education, of all places, are where people should learn about the value of intellectual property and the importance of protecting it.

Lawsuits Are the Last Resort

The fact that students continue to engage in this behavior is particularly egregious given the extraordinary lengths to which we have gone to address the problem. Our approach always has been and continues to be collaborative—partnering with and appealing to the higher motives of universities. We have met personally with university administrators. We have provided both instructional material and educational resources, including an orientation video to help deter illegal downloading. We have worked productively through organizations like

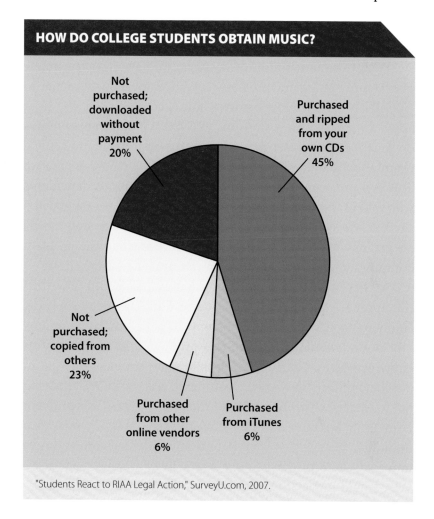

HOW DO COLLEGE STUDENTS OBTAIN MUSIC?

Not purchased; downloaded without payment 20%

Purchased and ripped from your own CDs 45%

Not purchased; copied from others 23%

Purchased from other online vendors 6%

Purchased from iTunes 6%

"Students React to RIAA Legal Action," SurveyU.com, 2007.

the Joint Committee of the Higher Education and Entertainment Communities. We have participated in Congressional hearings.

We have informed schools of effective network technologies to inhibit illegal activity. We have licensed legitimate music services at steeply discounted rates for college students and helped to arrange partnership opportunities between universities and legitimate services. We have stepped up our notice program to alert schools and students of infringing activity. And, of course, we have as a last resort brought suit against individual file-traffickers.

With this latest round of lawsuits, we have initiated a new pre-lawsuit settlement program intended to allow students to voluntarily settle claims before a suit is actually filed. We have asked for school administrations' assistance in passing our letters on to students in order to give them the opportunity to settle a claim at a discounted rate and before a public record is created. This is a program initiated in part as a response to defendants who told us they would like this opportunity, and we are encouraged by the swift response of so many schools. Lawsuits are by no means our desired course of action. But when the problem continues to persist, year after year, we are left with no choice.

An op-ed writer recently published in this forum described this approach as bullying. There is a big difference between using "bullying tactics" and using a "bully pulpit" to make an important point. Should we ignore this problem and stand silent as entire generations of students learn to steal? Should we not point out that administrators are brushing off responsibility, choosing not to exercise their moral leadership on this issue? This problem is anything but ours and ours alone. If music is stolen with such impunity, what makes term papers any different? Yet we know university administrators very aggressively pursue plagiarism. Why would universities—so prolific in the creation of intellectual capital themselves—not apply the same high standards to intellectual property of all kinds? This is, after all, a segment of our economy responsible for more than 6 percent of our nation's GDP [gross domestic product].

Furthermore, a Business Software Alliance study conducted last year found that 86 percent of managers say that the file-sharing attitudes and behaviors of applicants affect on their hiring decisions. Don't administrators have an obligation to prepare students for the real world, where theft is simply not tolerated? Our strategy is not to bully but to point out that the self-interest of universities lies remarkably close to the interests of the entertainment industries whose products are being looted. And, most importantly, we have sought to do so in a collaborative way.

Schools Must Step Up

It doesn't have to be like this. We take this opportunity to once again ask schools to be proactive, to step up and accept responsibility for the activity of their students on their network—not legal responsibility, but moral responsibility, as educators, as organizations transmitting values. Turning a blind eye will not make the problem go away; it will further ingrain in students the belief that a costly and illegal pastime is sanctioned, and even facilitated, by school administrations.

The necessary steps are simple. First, implement a network technical solution. Products like Red Lambda's cGrid are promising as effective and comprehensive solutions that maintain the integrity, security, and legal use of school computing systems without threatening student privacy. Some schools have used these products to block the use of P2P entirely, realizing that the overwhelming, if not sole, use of these applications on campus is to illegally download and distribute copyrighted works. For schools that do not wish to prohibit entirely access to P2P applications, products such as Audible Magic's CopySense can be used to filter illegal P2P traffic, again, without impinging on student privacy.

Second, offer a legal online service to give students an inexpensive alternative to stealing. One such service, Ruckus, is funded through advertising and is completely free to users. When schools increasingly provide their students with amenities like cable TV, there is simply no reason not to offer them cheap or free legal access to the music they crave.

Third, take appropriate and consistent disciplinary action when students are found to be engaging in infringing conduct online. This includes stopping and punishing such activity in dorms and on all Local Area Networks throughout a school's computing system.

Some administrations have embraced these solutions, engaged in productive dialogue with us to address this problem, and begun to see positive results. We thank these schools and commend them for their responsible actions.

Yet the vast majority of institutions still have not come to grips with the need to take appropriate action. As we continue our necessary enforcement measures—including our notices and pre-lawsuit settlement initiative—and as Congress continues to monitor this issue with a watchful eye, we hope these schools will fully realize the harm their inaction causes them and their students. We call upon them to do their part to address this continuing, mutual problem.

| *"I'm not saying that file-sharing is right.*
I'm not saying that it's wrong either.
What I'm saying is that file-sharing is."

A Student Discusses Being Sued for Illegal Music Downloading

Personal Narrative

Ernesto

The following viewpoint includes a discussion with Joel Tenenbaum, a Boston college student who was sued by the Recording Industry Association of America (RIAA) in 2007 for illegally downloading music and ordered by a jury to pay a fine of $675,000 (later reduced to $67,500). In the viewpoint, Tenenbaum contends that the amount of his fine was unfair, based not on the amount of damage actually caused to the RIAA but on their determination to make an example of him. In fact, he argues, while he does download music without paying for it, he often ends up purchasing the music after he listens to it, and therefore does not really harm musicians or their record labels. Ernesto is the founder and editor in chief of *the blog TorrentFreak, which explores the world of peer-to-peer file sharing.*

Boston student Joel Tenenbaum is the poster child of an entire generation of downloaders, and one of the few people to stand up against the RIAA [Recording Industry Association of America] instead of signing off on a settlement. This decision proved to be a costly one for Tenenbaum, who now has to pay $67,500 in damages to the record labels for sharing 7 songs. In an interview he now looks back at recent years.

The case of Boston student Joel Tenenbaum against the RIAA has been dragging on for half a decade already. Last year [2009], a jury found Tenenbaum guilty of "willful infringement" and awarded damages mounting to $675,000.

In July this year [2010] judge Nancy Gertner ruled that the penalty was excessive and unconstitutional and the jury-awarded damages were subsequently reduced by 90%.

Soon after this judgment both the RIAA and Tenenbaum appealed once again, and the case continues. Although many scholars, journalists and commenters have discussed this high profile case in detail over the years, Joel himself hasn't shared his thoughts that often.

But, for an introductory course on the production of digital media, Joel is opening up. Brett Caraway, a lecturer in the Department of Radio-Television-Film at the University of Texas informed TorrentFreak about the newly launched discussion platform on copyright issues. One of the first of many high profile individuals involved in recent P2P [peer-to-peer file sharing] litigation that is featured on the site is Joel Tenenbaum.

"The intention of the site is to bring together interested parties with various perspectives and have them interact with students and each other. It is my hope that my students and the public can find something of value in these discussions which will help them make up their own minds," Caraway told TorrentFreak.

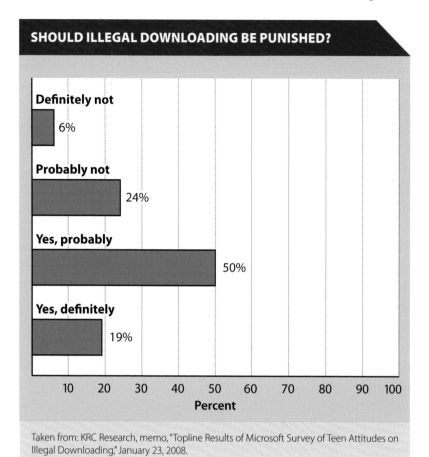

SHOULD ILLEGAL DOWNLOADING BE PUNISHED?

Definitely not
6%

Probably not
24%

Yes, probably
50%

Yes, definitely
19%

Percent

Taken from: KRC Research, memo, "Topline Results of Microsoft Survey of Teen Attitudes on Illegal Downloading," January 23, 2008.

With permission we're posting the interview with Joel Tenenbaum here. Those interested in discussions around copyright issues should keep a close eye on the Copy Grounds website. . . .

Joel Tenenbaum Interview

I download hundreds of songs every month from artists very few people know about that have a lot more to lose than the popular ones you downloaded from and I'm not going to get in trouble. Does that seem fair to you?

Joel: Well, no. It's not fair. Then again, it's not fair that out of 40,000 people who have been sued for file-sharing, I was the one who was lucky enough to have my parents behind me, Professor Charles Nesson and his colleagues, and dedicated passionate students working for free to help me out. I might be unlucky, but I'm also damn lucky for what I've been given and for who I have standing with me.

Did you plan to fight against the RIAA to this extent, or did it just slowly escalate into what it is today?

I didn't plan to fight at all. I wasn't looking to become the "poster child" for all file-sharers. I tried to settle—multiple times. I offered $500 from the outset and $5250 in court, but by then, this offer was apparently not enough for the music labels. And besides, the idea that someone could just call you up and ask you for thousands of dollars, showing no hard evidence, without your getting a fair day's representation in court seemed absurd.

What are you hoping to change by "fighting back" against the RIAA? Of course you understand that peer to peer file sharing has to be controlled in some way, so if it were up to you, how would the problem of file sharing be handled?

I'm not "hoping to change" anything. The RIAA sued me. I just want to have a fair day in court for the allegations against me. I'm not the one who can dismiss the lawsuit. Maybe the better question is: What are they hoping to change?

Has this ordeal changed the way people treat you?

Every time I appear in the *Metro* (the free Boston paper) all my friends and my graduate advisor get a kick out of it. Most people that recognize me are generally appreciative and tell me to stick with it. Thankfully, no one seems to be as hostile in person to me as I've seen on the internet.

Joel, I am curious as to whether your focus with your case is to argue simply that peer to peer file sharing is completely fair, or if you're arguing that the way the RIAA is approaching these cases is unjust? One of the questions I have for Joel Tenenbaum is, "What do you feel your punishment should be [for] illegally download-ing music and sharing files; do you believe you should face conse-quences at all?"

I'm not saying that file-sharing is right. I'm not saying that it's wrong either. What I'm saying is that file-sharing is. What I'm fighting in court is that $675,000—and even $67,500—for 30 songs is unjust. Turns out that you can NOT use a civil lawsuit to "deter" other individuals: it's an abuse of court. And so, "making an example" out of me to scare others is more than just unfair. I wouldn't be averse to some sort of penalty in line with 99 cents per song or somewhere remotely in that neighborhood if the RIAA can actually show harm, which they haven't.

If you somehow knew that this much of a fuss would be caused for downloading 7 songs, would you still do this to prove this point?

Complicated question, and a tempting one, I know. [American screenwriter] Charlie Kaufman writes, "There are a million little strings attached to every choice you make." I'm grateful for how things have gone. Had this not happened, I wouldn't have had the experiences I've had and met all the amazing people that I've met. But again, I'm not doing this to prove a point. I didn't start the lawsuit. They're the ones with a point to prove.

In your opinion, should lawsuits such as these even exist? In other words, do you even recognize what you did as wrong, or do you think that the RIAA is stepping outside of its bounds to prosecute?

I believe that the RIAA has the right to pursue what they believe they are entitled to under the law of the land just as I have the right to speak out against them and defend myself. That's the way our court system works. But the way the "scales of justice" are weighed down on their side; in a way, they get to buy more "justice" by having the deep pockets necessary to pay dozens of lawyers to fabricate an interpretation out of a statute we believe wasn't intended. They use raw power to silence anyone who dares say otherwise . . . that's an abuse of taxpayer money, resources, and one of the most respected justice systems in the world.

By and large, have netizens had a positive outlook on the case, or a negative one?

You can get a decent sense of the proportions just looking at the comments on our blog, YouTube videos, or the comments of the articles themselves. They seem to come out 5:1 in favor of us. I did a radio show and people called in: same comments, same ratio. The archetypes are:

- Screw the RIAA!!
- The reason the record companies aren't making money and people aren't buying is new music isn't worth paying for. No quality.
- Screw you, Joel Tenenbaum. You're a self-important thief trying to get out of taking responsibility.
- It's not right, but come on, everybody does it! $67,500 is not a fair punishment.
- Hi, I'm an artist and here are the contractual details on how the RIAA screws artists in their agreements. Keep downloading!

Why do you feel you have the right to these files? Do you not think you should support the artists that you think are good? Also, do you simply amass files that you rarely listen to, or do you get rid of what you don't like/want/need?

I like music. I like to listen to it. I listen to it the way everyone around me listens to it. I'm not pioneering a new distribution system that makes sure everyone can get music for free. I'm just jumping in the pool with everyone else. I also believe and have always believed that artists I derive enjoyment from deserve to be paid for their work. There's this image of me as the "FREE MUSIC" guy who refuses to pay on principle; that's just flat-out untrue. I often have bought music as a result of the free exploration I've done. In that respect, I'm much like the average downloader, who actually spends more money on music than people who don't download at all.

How does Joel envision the future of the music industry?

I hope it will be a vibrant place, full of sharing, creativity, and the ability for artists to connect straight to their fans without legal intervention. Other than that, I'll have to rely on the visionary expertise of John Perry Barlow, lyricist for the Grateful Dead, who's been around a lot longer than me, and has the benefit of greater perspective I don't. Barlow wrote:

- I will testify that the Internet, and peer-to-peer technology in particular, allow us to do that which we, as humans, fundamentally need to do: share.

- I will explain how digital technology has finally freed us from the physical medium of CDs and other increasingly antiquated mediums, how this conversion challenges conventional application and why this natural evolution should be welcomed.

- I will testify that the music industry will never be in danger because, the reasons which I would not presume to know with certainty, we as humans absolutely require music, and because in the music business as I know it, familiarity, not scarcity, creates value.

- I will explain why this means that the industry surrounding music will never cease to exist in some form.

> "When [hostile communication] rises to
> a criminal level ... prosecutors should
> have a tool at their disposal to allow
> them to punish the perpetrator."

Federal Laws Are Needed to Protect Young People from Cyberbullying

Linda Sánchez

Sánchez argues that the federal government should pass the Megan Meier Cyberbullying Prevention Act, a law she designed to prevent cyberbullying. Sánchez, whose viewpoint was originally presented as testimony before the US House of Representatives Subcommittee on Crime, Terrorism, and Homeland Security, describes the harmful effects of bullying, and explains how cyberbullying—or bullying conducted online or over cell phones—can be even more harmful than face-to-face contact, because it is often constant, public, and anonymous. The Act would make it a federal crime to issue "serious, repeated and hostile communications" with harmful intent. Sánchez, who was elected to the US Congress in 2003, proposed the bill in 2008 and 2009 but got little support from her colleagues, who feared the law would violate the First Amendment guarantees of free speech.

Linda Sánchez, Testimony Hearing on the Megan Meier Cyberbullying Prevention Act, US House Committee on the Judiciary, Subcommittee on Crime, Terrorism, and Homeland Security, September 30, 2009.

When I was first elected to Congress, I held a series of meetings with local school superintendents and law enforcement leaders to learn more about the challenges they face in helping to keep our children safe and on the right track.

I heard a recurring theme—that bullying is not a harmless prank or rite of passage. It is dangerous, both physically and mentally.

Bullying can lead to poor school performance, more absences, or even dropping out of school altogether.

The prospect of assault and harassment can lead a child to join a gang for protection. Not only can bullying cause physical injuries, including cuts, bruises, and broken bones, but it can also lead to depression, and even suicide.

This is why I have been working to change federal law so that schools can use federal funds to address and prevent bullying and harassment.

But, over the last several years, I have learned that this approach isn't enough.

Bullying has gone electronic. It occurs in text messages and G-Chat; on Facebook and MySpace; on cell phones and the internet.

This literally means that kids can be bullied any hour of the day or night and *even in their own homes.*

Today's kids are so wired into their electronic social networks that they type more messages than they speak each day. Their virtual world is more *real* to them than the so-called real world.

For those of us over 30, this can be difficult to comprehend. Let me give you an example to illustrate the problem.

Imagine if, in our day, a student brought a big TV out to the quad and played for the entire student body a videotape in which he threatened and harassed a second student. By the end of the day, everyone, and I mean everyone, would have seen or heard about it.

Tina Meier holds photos of her daughter Megan, who committed suicide in 2007 after receiving cruel messages on MySpace. © AP Images/Tom Gannam.

Well, that's exactly what cyberbullying is. Because of the anonymity and deception the internet allows, this form of bullying is particularly dangerous.

If Bobby posts a video on his Facebook page that harasses and threatens to rape and kill Ashley, that video isn't private. It's not buried on Bobby's profile page somewhere.

It's public. It appears when any of Bobby's Facebook friends log in—right there up front on their home page, so they can't miss it.

Tragic Examples

This story isn't just a hypothetical. It happened to a brave young woman named Hail Ketchum-Wiggins, who lives in Southern California, near my Congressional district.

And similar bullying incidents are happening every day to young people across our nation.

Cyberbullying is always mean, ill mannered, and cruel. But some cyberbullying is so harmful that it rises to the level of criminal behavior.

My bill, the Megan Meier Cyberbullying Prevention Act, is named to honor a young woman who was the victim of just such criminal behavior.

Three years ago [in 2006], 13-year-old Megan Meier of Missouri hung herself after being tormented and harassed by her 15-year-old MySpace friend "Josh." "Josh" told her, among other things, "The world would be better off without you."

Eventually, Megan's family learned that "Josh" was really a creation of Lori Drew [the mother of Megan's classmate].

Local prosecutors in Missouri couldn't bring charges against Lori Drew because, at the time, Missouri had no law to punish such cruelty.

A federal prosecutor, in a similar bind, got creative and charged Drew with computer fraud. Even though the jury convicted her, the judge threw out the conviction [in 2009].

The result is that Drew, an adult, and one who should have been setting an example of good behavior, will never be punished for her outrageous behavior toward her 13-year-old victim, Megan.

CYBERBULLYING VICTIMIZATION

In a 2010 survey of 4,441 youths between the ages of 10 and 18 from a large school district in the southern United States, more than 20 percent said that they had been the victims of cyberbullying.

| ■ Lifetime | □ Previous 30 days |

I have been cyberbullied (lifetime)
20.8%

I have been cyberbullied
7.5%

Mean or hurtful comments online
14.3%

Rumors online
13.3%

Threatened to hurt me through a cell phone text
8.4%

Threatened to hurt me online
7.2%

Pretended to be me online
6.7%

Posted a mean or hurtful picture of me online
5.0%

One or more, two or more times
17.0%

10 20 30 40 50 60 70 80 90 100
Percent

Taken from: Sameer Hinduja, and Justin W. Patchin, Cyberbullying Research Center, 2010.

These are just brief examples of why Congress needs to address new crimes like cyberbullying.

Words that didn't exist just a couple of years ago, including "sexting," and "textual harassment," describe the new ways people use technology to hurt, harass, and humiliate each other. When these behaviors become serious, repeated, and hostile, we can no longer ignore them.

While Missouri has since enacted a cyberbullying statute, the children of other states are waiting for Congress to act. That is why I am grateful that the Committee is considering the Megan Meier Cyberbullying Prevention Act.

A Constitutional Prohibition on Cyberbullying Is Possible

Before I conclude, I want to acknowledge how difficult it will be to craft a prohibition on cyberbullying that is consistent with the Constitution. But I also believe that working together for our children, we can and must do so.

The Supreme Court has already recognized that some regulation of speech is consistent with the First Amendment. For example, the Court has approved restrictions on true threats, obscenities, and some commercial speech. But it has been more hostile to attempts to limit political speech.

I do not intend anything in the Megan Meier Cyberbullying Prevention Act to override Supreme Court jurisprudence.

Instead, I want the law to be able to distinguish between an annoying chain e-mail, a righteously angry political blog post, or a miffed text to an ex-boyfriend—all of which are and should remain legal—and serious, repeated, and hostile communications made with the intent to harm.

When the latter rises to a criminal level, as it did in the case of Lori Drew, prosecutors should have a tool at their disposal to allow them to punish the perpetrator.

I believe that we can protect our right to free speech *and* victims of cyberbullying at the same time.

I look forward to working with colleagues on both sides of the aisle to do so.

I thank you for the opportunity to testify today and hope that you will all join me in supporting this legislation.

> *"In a perfect world, we could legislate niceness, but this world is far from perfect."*

Making Cyberbullying Illegal Unnecessarily Limits Free Speech

WebProNews Staff

In the following viewpoint, an unnamed staff writer for the website WebProNews.com argues that the Megan Meier Cyberbullying Prevention Act—under consideration by Congress in 2009 when the viewpoint was published—is a well-meaning but dangerous attempt to protect victims from bullying. The language of the bill, according to the viewpoint, is so vague that it could be interpreted to include many kinds of speech that might be impassioned or angry but do not rise to the level of abuse. Bullying is a sad fact of life, the writer concludes, but to violate the freedom of speech guaranteed by the First Amendment would be a greater harm. WebProNews is an online resource for news, information, and tips related to online business.

I always thought that of all the amendments to the U.S. Constitution, the first one was both the most memorable and the easiest to understand: You can say what you like, outside of the famous "shouting fire" example, and the government can't stop you. Easy. A toddler could get it.

(My mother taught civics/law and justice for 25 years, and I assure you that when your humble author was a toddler he understood the First Amendment.)

But U.S. Representative Linda Sánchez (D-CA) and 14 other House members are grownups smart enough to get themselves elected to Congress, and they still don't get it? Sánchez, with 14 co-sponsors, has reintroduced the Megan Meier Cyberbullying Prevention Act, which reads:

> "Whoever transmits in interstate or foreign commerce any communication, with the intent to coerce, intimidate, harass, or cause substantial emotional distress to a person, using electronic means to support severe, repeated, and hostile behavior, shall be fined under this title or imprisoned not more than two years, or both."

By "electronic means" they mean: any equipment dependent on electrical power to access an information service, including e-mail, instant messaging, blogs, websites, telephones, and text messages.

So, that's 15 U.S. representatives who either don't understand or are unfamiliar with the First Amendment to the U.S. Constitution. Maybe we should bring my mother out of retirement and require all of our representatives to take her ninth grade civics class before writing legislation.

The bill is named for the poor girl who committed suicide after being harassed online by a classmate's mother. Though no one (I hope) sympathizes with the heinous actions of Lori Drew, Sánchez should be roundly harangued for exploiting a child's sad story to manipulate the heartstrings of other legislators to the point Congress passes a law abridging freedom of speech.

See what I did there? If I said that twice, if Sánchez's feelings were hurt, and a court judged my statement "severe," I'd be a felon facing two years in prison. I haven't said anything especially vicious, just harshly criticized a politician on the Internet, but the problem with this cyberbullying legislation is that words like *coercion, intimidate, harass, emotional stress, severe,* and *hostile* are subject to vast differences in interpretation.

Too Vague to Be Administered Fairly

Eugene Volokh, professor of law at UCLA School of Law, outlines six ways this law could be abused, which I'll paraphrase as follows:

1. Repeatedly petitioning (harassing) a politician via e-mail using potentially hostile or severe words (hypocrite, fool, traitor).

2. Blogs and editorials repeatedly using the same type of language as above.

3. Shaming a public figure (intending to cause substantial emotional distress).

4. Repeatedly and angrily e-mailing a company that refuses to refund money owed.

5. Online boycotts and petitions.

6. Angry e-mails from a wife to a husband who cheated on her.

It's potentially limitless the situations to which this language could apply. Though not expressly mentioned in the definition of "electronic means," the atrociously loose definition could also apply to TV and radio.

A critic in response may argue such scenarios are highly unlikely, but hardly a day goes by I don't see a story of authority abusing its power for its own reasons. An Orlando police chief threatening a blogger with a defamation suit, his attorney asserting the "truth is not always a defense" in the process, comes to mind. An Alaskan politician outing an anonymous blogger for revenge is another example (talk about cyberbullying!). The ways authority figures have abused their powers are far too numerous to list.

Cyberbullying can be more harmful than a physical confrontation because of its ability to reach a broad audience. Some argue that both are a regrettable fact of life. © Henry King/ Photonica/Getty Images.

In June 2008, the first time Sánchez tried to introduce this legislation (it never came to a vote before the previous session ended), Volokh succinctly addresses the broadness of the language:

> "Its reference to blogs and websites strongly suggests that it deliberately addresses one-to-many publishing media as well as one-to-one e-mail and text messaging—but even without that reference, it would literally cover any 'communication,' with no limitation that the communication be sent specifically to the distressed person."

Yep, even Twitter. No mean tweeting allowed.

Even more succinct is C.J. Ciaramella, of the *Oregon Communicator*: "Rep. Sánchez seems to believe that it aught to be illegal to make someone feel bad."

Let me be even more succinct: good intentions don't always make good law.

Cyberbullying, like bullying before there were various electronic means to conduct it, is an unfortunate fact of life, like viruses and skinned knees. I would like to protect my daughter from all those things forever, but I also know that her having to deal with them eventually will make her a stronger, more unflappable adult (who also knows Daddy's ready to kick some tail if necessary!). In a perfect world, we could legislate niceness, but this world is far from perfect, no matter how much padding we put down to protect our little darlings' noggins and shins.

This bill is currently [2009] under review by the House Judiciary Committee, where, even if committee members appreciate the intent, it will likely meet its Constitutional end [the bill was not acted on]. One imagines at least a few on the Judiciary Committee have taken a ninth grade civics course. If not, God help us.

Organizations to Contact

The editors have compiled the following list of organizations concerned with the issues debated in this book. The descriptions are derived from materials provided by the organizations. All have publications or information available for interested readers. The list was compiled on the date of publication of the present volume; the information provided here may change. Be aware that many organizations take several weeks or longer to respond to queries, so allow as much time as possible.

American Center for Law and Justice (ACLJ)
PO Box 90555
Washington, DC 20090-0555
(800) 296-4529
website: http://aclj.org

The American Center for Law and Justice (ACLJ) focuses on constitutional law, specifically the ideal it ascribes to that religious freedom and freedom of speech are inalienable, God-given rights. The organization has participated in numerous cases regarding student education rights and the freedom of parents to make decisions about their children's education and has supported efforts to increase Internet filtering in public libraries and to punish those who make Internet pornography available to young people. Its website provides radio and television feeds, podcasts, photos, news releases, and commentaries, as well as legal briefs on topics including "Pornography on the Internet and in the Community" and "Overview of Student Constitutional Rights."

American Civil Liberties Union (ACLU)
125 Broad Street
18th Floor
New York, NY 10004

(212) 549-2500
e-mail: infoaclu@aclu.org
website: www.aclu.org

Founded in 1920, the ACLU is a nonprofit and nonpartisan organization of more than 500,000 members and supporters. The mission of the ACLU is to preserve all of the protections and guarantees of the US Constitution's Bill of Rights, and the organization has been involved in several Supreme Court cases concerning teens' Internet rights. The ACLU's Technology and Liberty Program monitors the interplay between cutting-edge technology and civil liberties, actively promoting responsible uses of technology that enhance privacy and freedom, while opposing those that it believes undermine freedom and move closer to a surveillance society. Its website has a collection of news articles, as well as a blog, newsfeeds, podcasts, and "Stand Up with the ACLU," a section dedicated to youth issues. Publications include legal and legislative facts sheets and reports, and articles about online free speech.

American Library Association

50 E. Huron Street
Chicago, IL 60611
(800) 545-2433
website: www.ala.org

Founded in 1876, the American Library Association (ALA) provides leadership for the development, promotion, and improvement of library and information services and the profession of librarianship in order to enhance learning and ensure access to information for all. Its website offers extensive information about intellectual freedom issues, including Internet filtering, censorship and First Amendment issues, the Children's Internet Protection Act, and privacy and confidentiality. The ALA also publishes a Library Bill of Rights, outlining the role of public libraries in providing material for all patrons.

Electronic Frontier Foundation (EFF)

454 Shotwell Street
San Francisco, CA 94110-1914
(415) 436-9333
website: www.eff.org
e-mail: information@eff.org

The Electronic Frontier Foundation (EFF) is a donor-funded nonprofit organization of lawyers, policy analysts, activists, and technologists who work to defend free speech, privacy, innovation, and consumer rights. EFF fights for freedom primarily in the courts, bringing and defending lawsuits against the US government or large corporations. The group also produces educational and advocacy materials for policymakers, the press and public. Its website includes a blog, information about court cases argued by the group, and articles and reports including "Peer-to-Peer File Sharing and Copyright Law: A Primer for Developers" and "Know Your Digital Rights." EFF sponsors an extensive "Teaching Copyright" site at www.teachingcopyright.org/resources.

Electronic Privacy Information Center (EPIC)

1718 Connecticut Avenue NW
Suite 200
Washington, DC 20009
(202) 483-1140
website: http://epic.org

EPIC, a public interest research center in Washington, DC, was established in 1994 to focus public attention on emerging civil liberties issues and to protect privacy, the First Amendment, and constitutional values. EPIC publishes the *EPIC Alert*, an award-winning e-mail and online newsletter on civil liberties in the information age, as well as reports and books about privacy, open government, free speech, and other important topics related to civil liberties. Its website includes extensive analysis and documentation of privacy issues including the Children's Online

Privacy Protection Act (COPPA), gender and electronic privacy, and social networking.

First Amendment Center

John Seigenthaler Center at Vanderbilt University
1207 18th Avenue S.
Nashville, TN 37212
(615) 727-1600
e-mail: info@fac.org
website: www.firstamendmentcenter.org

The First Amendment Center supports the First Amendment and builds understanding of its core freedoms through education, information and entertainment. The center is nonpartisan and does not lobby or litigate. Its website features daily updates on news about First Amendment-related developments as well as information and detailed reports about US Supreme Court cases involving the First Amendment and commentary, analysis, and special reports involving free expression, press freedom, cyberspeech, blogging, hate speech online, and filtering.

Legal Information Institute (LII)

Cornell University
Ithaca, NY 14853
website: www.law.cornell.edu

The Legal Information Institute, a not-for-profit organization that believes everyone should be able to read and understand the laws that govern them, is a small research, engineering, and editorial group housed at the Cornell Law School in Ithaca, New York. Its collaborators include publishers, legal scholars, computer scientists, government agencies, and other groups and individuals that promote open access to law, worldwide. The group gathers and publishes primary documents online, creates materials that help people understand law, and explores new technologies that make it easier for people to find the law.

National Coalition Against Censorship (NCAC)

275 7th Avenue, #1504
New York, NY 10001
(212) 807-6222 • fax: (212) 807-6245
e-mail: ncac@ncac.org
website: www.ncac.org

The National Coalition Against Censorship (NCAC), founded in 1974, is an alliance of 50 national literary, artistic, religious, educational, professional, labor, and civil liberties groups. NCAC works to educate the public about the dangers of censorship and how to oppose it and includes Internet and sexual orientation issues among its focus areas. It sponsors the Youth Free Expression Network (YFEN), which provides speakers and films. Its website features articles and reports including "The Kids Are Online: Six Myths About Youth and Social Media," "Internet Filters in Schools and Libraries," and "Student Speech Online: Can or Should Schools Punish It?"

National Youth Rights Association (NYRA)

1101 15th Street NW, Suite 200
Washington, DC 20005
(202) 835-1739
website: www.youthrights.org

NYRA is a youth-led nonprofit organization dedicated to fighting for the civil rights and liberties of young people. NYRA works to lower the voting age, lower the drinking age, repeal curfew laws, protect student rights, and fight against ageism. Among NYRA's publications available on its website is "Analysis of US Curfew Laws."

SafeLibraries.org

641 Shunpike Road, #123
Chatham, NJ 07928
e-mail: SafeLibraries@gmail.com
website: www.SafeLibraries.org

SafeLibraries.org is dedicated to protecting children and families from dangerous policies of the American Library Association (ALA). Specifically, SafeLibraries.org opposes many of the ALA's recommendations about the age-appropriateness of individual books, its positions on censorship, and its resistance to Internet filtering in public libraries. Safe Libraries encourages the passage of state Internet filtering laws and local ordinances nationwide, and its website includes an extensive page detailing state and city Children's Internet Protection Act (CIPA) laws in all fifty states. Its website offers a SafeLibraries blog, articles about good and bad library practices, videos from local and national news programs, and links to other organizations and reports.

Student Press Law Center (SPLC)

1101 Wilson Boulevard, Suite 1100
Arlington, VA 22209-2275
(703) 807-1904
website: www.splc.org

The Student Press Law Center (SPLC), a nonprofit, non-partisan corporation, is the nation's only legal assistance agency devoted exclusively to educating high school and college journalists about the rights and responsibilities embodied in the First Amendment and supporting student news media in their struggle to cover important issues free from censorship. The Center provides free legal advice and information as well as low-cost educational materials for student journalists. Online materials include a "Student Media Guide to Internet Law," the "SPLC Guide to Off-Campus Web Sites," "Understanding Cybershield Law" and "Responding to Takedown Demands."

Supreme Court of the United States

Public Information Officer
Supreme Court of the United States
1 First Street, NE

Washington, DC 20543
website: www.supremecourt.gov

The Supreme Court is the highest court in the United States, and its opinions are considered final and binding unless the Supreme Court itself reverses one of its own decisions. The Court's website posts full-text copies of recent opinions, dissents and arguments, and includes information for locating and obtaining older decisions.

For Further Reading

Books

Fred H. Cate, *The Internet and the First Amendment: Schools and Sexually Explicit Expression*. Bloomington, IN: Phi Delta Kappa Educational Foundation, 1998.

Ronald Delbert, *Access Denied: The Practice and Policy of Global Internet Filtering*. Cambridge, MA: MIT Press, 2008.

Nathan W. Fisk, *Understanding Online Piracy: The Truth About Illegal File Sharing*. Santa Barbara, CA: Praeger, 2009.

Mike Godwin, *Cyber Rights: Defending Free Speech in the Digital Age*. New York: Times Books, 1998.

Jack L. Goldsmith and Tim Wu, *Who Controls the Internet?: Illusions of a Borderless World*. New York: Oxford University Press, 2006.

Sherri Mabry Gordon, *Downloading Copyrighted Stuff from the Internet: Stealing or Fair Use?* Berkeley Heights, NJ: Enslow Publishers, 2005.

Maureen Harrison and Steve Gilbert, *Obscenity and Pornography Decisions of the United States Supreme Court*. Carlsbad, CA: Excellent Books, 2000.

Constance S. Hawke, *Computer and Internet Use on Campus: A Legal Guide to Issues of Intellectual Property, Free Speech, and Privacy*. San Francisco, CA: Jossey-Bass, 2001.

Marjorie Heins, *Not in Front of the Children: "Indecency," Censorship and the Innocence of Youth*. New York: Hill and Wang, 2001.

Sameer Hinduja and Justin W. Patchin, *Bullying Beyond the Schoolyard: Preventing and Responding to Cyberbullying*. Thousand Oaks, CA: Sage, 2009.

David L. Hudson, *The Silencing of Student Voices: Preserving Free Speech in America's Schools*. Nashville, TN: First Amendment Center, 2003.

Thomas A. Jacobs, *Teen Cyberbullying Investigated: Where Do Your Rights End and Consequences Begin?* Minneapolis, MN: Free Spirit Publishing, 2010.

Margaret C. Jasper, *Privacy and the Internet: Your Expectations and Rights Under the Law*. New York: Oceana, 2009.

Ken Knapton, *Cyber Safety: Maintaining Morality in a Digital World*. Springville, UT: CFI, 2009.

Robin Kowalski and Susan Limber, *Cyber Bullying: Bullying in the Digital Age*. Maiden, MA: Blackwell, 2008.

Saul X. Levmore and Martha Craven Nussbaum, *The Offensive Internet: Speech, Privacy, and Reputation*. Cambridge, MA: Harvard University Press, 2010.

John Logie, *Peers, Pirates, and Persuasion: Rhetoric in the Peer-to-Peer Debates*. Anderson, SC: Parlor Press, 2006.

Michael Rustad, *Internet Law in a Nutshell*. St. Paul, MN: West, 2009.

Shaheen Shariff, *Confronting Cyber-bullying: What Schools Need to Know to Control Misconduct and Avoid Legal Consequences*. New York: Cambridge University Press, 2009.

Lynn Sutton, *Access Denied: How Internet Filters Impact Student Learning in High Schools*. Amherst, NY: Cambria Press, 2006.

Don Tapscott, *Growing Up Digital: The Rise of the Net Generation*. New York: McGraw-Hill, 1998.

Nancy Willard, *Cyberbullying and Cyberthreats: Responding to the Challenge of Online Social Aggression, Threats, and Distress*. Champaign, IL: Research Press, 2007.

Periodicals and Internet Sources

Emily Bazelon, "The Ninny State: The Danger of Overprotecting Your Kids from Technology," *New York Times,* June 26, 2011.

Kevin P. Brady, "Lifting the Limits on Social Networking Sites," *School Administrator,* February 2010.

Antony Bruno, "New Sheriff in Town: Anti-piracy Company's Shifting Tactics Reflect Market's Pivot from Enforcement to Engagement," *Billboard,* July 9, 2011.

John Cloud, "When Bullying Turns Deadly: Can It Be Stopped?" *Time,* October 24, 2010.

Alex Gomez, "Students, Officials Locking Horns over Blogs," *USA Today,* November 26, 2006.

Chandra M. Hayslett, "Music Pirates Going Overboard! Artists Fight Back to Protect Their Livelihoods," *Black Enterprise,* February 2007.

Marjorie Heins, Christina Cho and Ariel Feldman, "Internet Filters: A Public Policy Report," Brennan Center for Justice, 2006. www.fepproject.org.

Julie Hilden, "Government Should Stay Out of the Internet," *Los Angeles Daily Journal,* July 9, 2004.

Elizabeth Blanks Hindman, "Protecting Childhood: Rights, Social Goals and the First Amendment in the Context of the Child Online Protection Act," *Communication Law and Policy,* vol. 15, no. 1, 2010, pp. 1–23.

"Internet Access Is a 'Fundamental Right,'" *BBC News,* March 8, 2010. http://news.bbc.co.uk.

Wendy Kaminer, "Screen Saviors," *American Prospect,* June 4, 2001.

Elizabeth Kirby and Brenda Kaillio, "Student Blogs Mark a New Frontier for School Discipline," *Education Digest,* January 2007.

David Kravets, "Copyright Lawsuits Plummet in Aftermath of RIAA Campaign," Wired.com, May 18, 2010.

Richard Laliberte, "Testing the Limits: Your Teen's Legal Rights," *Family Circle,* January 2011.

Fonda Marie Lloyd, "Is It Wise to Censor the Net? Legislation Raises Questions About Freedom of Speech and Decency," *Black Enterprise,* December 1995.

Farhad Manjoo, "Can Anyone Stop the Music Cops?" Salon.com, June 17, 2003.

Michael Mayday, "High School Students Win Free Speech Cases," *Daily Caller,* June 15, 2011. http://dailycaller.com.

John F. McManus, "Internet Freedom Targeted," *New American,* January 18, 2010.

Jon Pareles, "Pay What You Want for This Article," *New York Times,* December 9, 2007.

Rahul Parikh, "Our Overblown Paranoia About the Internet and Teens," Salon.com, May 16, 2011.

Neil J. Rubenking, "Block Those Baddies," *PC Magazine,* March 21, 2006.

Linda Sánchez, "Protecting Victims, Preserving Freedoms," *Huffington Post,* May 6, 2009. www.huffingtonpost.com.

Deborah J. Thomas, "2009 School Safety Index: Cyber Security Not up to Par," KeepSchoolsSafe.org, May 18, 2009.

Andrew Trotter, "Administrators Confounded by Internet Pranks," *Education Week,* May 13, 1998.

Mary Elizabeth Williams, "The Case That Could End Cyberbullying," Salon.com, October 18, 2010.

Tim Wu, "The Future of Free Speech," *Chronicle of Higher Education*, November 19, 2010.

Index